ALLAN BATEMAN

MAINSTREAM / SPORT

ALLAN BATEMAN

THERE AND BACK AGAIN

ALLAN BATEMAN with PAUL REES

MAINSTREAM
PUBLISHING

EDINBURGH AND LONDON

To Nicola, Naomi and my parents.

First published in Great Britain in 2001 by
MAINSTREAM PUBLISHING COMPANY (EDINBURGH) LTD
7 Albany Street
Edinburgh EH1 3UG

This edition, 2002

ISBN 1 84018 668 2

A catalogue record for this book is available
from the British Library

Typeset in Caslon and Gothic
Printed and bound in Great Britain by
Cox & Wyman Ltd

ACKNOWLEDGEMENTS

The authors thank the following for their help in the preparation of this book: Nicola Bateman, Naomi Bateman, Lena Lewis, Dennis Bateman, Phillip Bateman, David Bateman, Linda Lewis, Brian Lewis; David Chadwick, Debbie Chadwick; Peter Williams; Dennis Thomas of Maesteg RFC; Jen Gadsby Peet of Richmond FC; Janet Hill; Alan Edmunds and Paul Abbandonato of *Wales on Sunday*; Peter Pace of *The Mirror*; and David Llewellyn of *The Independent*.

CONTENTS

ONE

ALL FOR LENA

Mothers knows best, or so they say. As a 15-year-old schoolboy with dreams of playing for Manchester United, I was not so sure. I needed a new pair of boots but my mother, Lena, would only delve into her purse on one condition.

'The boots will be for playing rugby in,' she said. 'Not soccer.' Definitely not soccer. My mum was a supporter of Bridgend RFC, even though they were the bitter rivals to our home town club, Maesteg. She liked going to the Brewery Field in Bridgend to see the likes of J.P.R. Williams and Steve Fenwick and, while I am not sure that she ever harboured ambitions of me playing first-class rugby, Manchester United and Old Trafford meant nothing to her. I had made up my mind to stop playing rugby and concentrate on soccer but Mum proved as formidable as any opponent I have since encountered on the field.

Not that I would ever have made it to Old Trafford. I was an enthusiastic rather than talented soccer player, more Nobby Stiles than Ryan Giggs. Even though I grew up in an era when Welsh rugby had never had it so good, I was more interested in doing than watching. The first time I saw Maesteg play was when I made my debut for them in 1984; I had only been to Bridgend once, in 1978, when they took on New Zealand. Internationals were different because a ticket for a Wales match carried kudos and, as my father Dennis was heavily involved in running the Maesteg Youth side, there were few international matches at the Arms Park that I missed.

I have never been a sports fan, which must sound strange given that rugby has been my livelihood since 1990. I must be one of the few men who subscribes to Sky but does not take any of its sport stations. There is too much soccer on television, too much sport on television. I still follow Manchester United, and when I played rugby league for Warrington for five years in the 1990s, I saw a number of matches at Old Trafford, but there is a world of difference between being at a sporting event and watching it on the box. Give me the real thing every time.

Sport is something I can take or leave – give me a good book any time - and yet I signed a two-year contract with Neath in 2001 which will take me past my 38th birthday. I will have been playing first-class rugby for 20 years, and for someone who was not driven by desire and ambition as a boy as far as rugby was concerned, it is not something I can properly explain. It seems as if my whole career has been an accident, a series of events where things fortunately fell into place. I am often asked about the secret of my longevity as a rugby player, a career which is increasingly being seen as a young man's occupation with the ever more intense physical demands of the game. There isn't one. My diet is probably the worst of any international player (chips with everything and forget the pasta), I am not teetotal and my life does not revolve around the sport. There is an obsession about age, as if once you have passed 30 you are no longer the player you were and, like a car that has reached 100,000 miles, the next stop is the scrapyard. When I returned home early from Wales's tour of Japan in 2001 because of an ankle injury, it was assumed by many that my international career was over because, at the age of 36, I was too old – but it should be about how well you are playing and not whether you are in the second half of your allotted three score years and ten.

Sport is not just about the physical but also the mental and where I have been lucky is that I have not had to live in a goldfish bowl in full view of the media. I have largely been able to pursue my career without being built up to be knocked down. When I joined Warrington from Neath in 1990, I was following a well-worn path and there was a widespread resentment up north about the legion of carpet-baggers from Wales who made their way up the M6 for financial gain without knowing much about the 13-a-side code except that it was professional. Many are the stories about Welshmen being snubbed by their own team-mates and set on by opponents. I never had any bother: there had been no fanfare announcing my arrival, my face and name were not widely known and I was allowed to settle in at my own pace, unfêted and barely announced. In cricket terms, I have been like a batsman who quietly accumulates with the opposition surprised to see that he has 70 or 80 to his name as opposed to a swashbuckler who peppers the outfield with an array of shots. Stealth has been my watchword.

I have been in the shadows for most of my career and that is how I would have planned it. It has been an advantage to have been out in Wales for so long because, in Warrington and then with Cronulla, Richmond and Northampton, it was not difficult to melt into the background. Wales is a rugby village where it is impossible to walk down a street without someone recognising you and wanting to talk about rugby. After Wales had lost heavily to England in 1998, 2000 and 2001, I did not have to face the recriminations, tucked away as I was in England. Long before the end of the 2001 season, a number of the leading Wales players were talking about retiring from international rugby. It was not that they were approaching the end of their careers – they were all far younger than me. It was more that years of being in the limelight, of being praised one minute and then decried as past it or over-rated the next, had taken their toll. Players invariably arouse mixed emotions: for every supporter or pundit who thinks you are the best thing since sliced bread, there is another who reckons you are not up to it and while there are players who are able to cope with the slings and arrows of fickle opinion, there are others who feel the pain.

Most players have a career graph which is full of ups and downs, highs and lows. Mine has been level and that has allowed me to enjoy a generally low profile. It has also probably extended my career and when I decided to return to Neath for the 2001–02 season, I did so partly because I expected that my international career would come to an end. Not that I will ever announce my retirement from Test rugby. I want to play at the highest level for as long as I can and, like a batsman who refuses to walk, I will wait for the umpire's decision. Sport is about today, not yesterday or tomorrow. You never know what is around the corner and while I may think that I have played my last game for Wales, I will never say never again.

I can understand why players call it a day on the international front only to continue at club level. Professionalism has led to several changes in rugby union, most of them for the better, but the demands of Test rugby can drive you out of your mind. It is not the playing, far from it, but the routine that goes with it: the travelling, in and out of airports and hotels, and the strict training regime with the lengthy lists of dos and don'ts. At times it is like being back at school and the repetitive routine gets to you. You are cloistered for days on end with the same group of men, talking trivia for the most part, and your whole day is mapped out for you. I like my freedom and the thought of the Wales squad spending the entire Six Nations campaign together, as has been suggested for the 2002 campaign, is more than I could bear. Perhaps it is just as well that my career is winding towards its conclusion because there is less scope for individualism today, with the emphasis on conformity.

I have been surprised at what I have achieved. There have been a number of times in my career when I was close to giving up rugby: halfway through my time with Maesteg at the end of the 1980s when players who were my contemporaries or younger were breaking into the Wales squad while I was getting nowhere; in 1995 when Warrington offered me a new contract which I felt was derisory and insulting; and in 1999 when the Richmond club collapsed and ended up being cannibalised (along with our tenants at the Athletic Ground, London Scottish) by the rest of the sides in the English first division – an act of betrayal which reflected poorly on rugby union in this country. When London Wasps hit financial problems in 2001, they approached Richmond, who had returned to their amateur roots and were playing several divisions below the Zurich Premiership, and asked if they would be interested in buying the club, or rather the club's considerable debts, for just one pound and getting back into the big time. Richmond, understandably, turned down the offer.

There is a saying in sport, handed down by the late Bill Shankly, that it is not about life or death; it is more important than that. It is not a view I have ever shared and one of the weaknesses of rugby in Wales is that there is too often a lack of perspective. Like a shower which is either too hot or too cold, Wales are either world-beaters or half the team should be dropped, depending on the latest result. Having experienced death at first hand, I long ago learned to distinguish between the essential and the superficial.

I had just turned 18 and had passed my driving test. For more than seven years I had lived with my grandmother on Mum's side, moving in with her after the death of my grandfather. Gran had a flat in Caerau, close to Mum's house where I had lived with my brothers Phillip and David. My parents had divorced when I was four and they both remarried. My stepfather, Brian Lewis, played a big part in my development as a rugby player, taking me to matches and always encouraging me.

I went to live with Gran to keep her company. One day in 1983, I was driving her to my auntie's in Crickhowell. Gran was in the back seat and when we reached Hirwaun, not far from Merthyr, I heard a noise and when I turned round Gran was struggling for breath. She was drifting in and out of consciousness and I became scared out of my mind. I suspected that she was having a heart attack and I tried to figure out where the nearest hospital was. I took her to the Prince Charles Hospital but there was nothing they could do for her and she died shortly after we arrived. To this day, I am convinced that she hung on so I would not see her die, but the experience was a traumatic one and it took me a long time to get over it. Even now my memories of that morning, when the minutes turned to hours, are still vivid.

Gran was only in her early 60s and she had not had a history of illness. She liked a cigarette and, mindful of the fact that I hated smoking, she would never light up in front of me and would lean out of a window when the craving took her even though it was her own flat. After Gran's death, David moved into the flat with me and he was to follow me into the Neath team. Whereas Phillip showed little sporting prowess, I always thought that David was the most able of the three of us but he was not driven by the desire to get to the top. He was a useful player who could play at either outside-half or in the centre, but he never achieved as much as he should have and a succession of injuries ended his career prematurely.

Phillip has been my most loyal supporter, quick to take offence if anyone says anything against me, while David is more objective. My family always make it to Cardiff on international days and they were out in force when I won my first Wales cap in 1990. I found out afterwards that they had taken part in a BBC Radio Wales programme which was broadcast live in the centre of Cardiff with Mum to the fore. I still do not know what was said – which, I am told, is just as well.

I have reached the stage in my career now when I am playing alongside or against the sons of men I used to play alongside or against. I was at a Wales training session during the 2000–01 season and started talking with a ginger-haired youngster who was regarded as a promising prospect in the centre. I asked him his name and when he replied Steve Winn I asked if he was any relation to Alan Winn, a former team-mate of mine at Maesteg Celtic back in 1984–5. 'I am his son,' he replied. I should be gone by the time the grandson comes of age.

Age is all in the mind. I think that I have prolonged my career by not staying too long at any one club. I have played for Maesteg, Neath, Richmond and Northampton in rugby union – and Warrington and Cronulla in rugby league. I have spent an average of three years at any one club and I could never imagine spending my entire career in the same place (I would stagnate) but I have always seen out my contracts, apart from my stay in Australia which ended prematurely because of family problems.

I have never played for Llanelli, but they came close to signing me on three occasions. The first was when I joined Neath in 1989, the second was when I left Cronulla and the third was in 2001 after I had decided to return to Neath from Northampton who had only offered me a one-year extension to my contract. Each time, Llanelli rang me just days after I had agreed to a move. I had not committed myself in writing, but my word is my bond and there was no going back. Some things are just not meant to be, but I always fancied playing in the red of Llanelli, a club with a great tradition. I had the chance of joining Cardiff, but that was a club which never appealed to me. The perception I had of them (and this could be totally unfair) was that they were a club who signed players for signing's sake, collecting individuals rather than building a team.

Close friends of mine play, and have played, for Cardiff, but the essence of a successful team to me is camaraderie. I have never played in a closer squad than Neath at the end of the 1980s. They were then probably the best club in Britain, armed with a fanatical support and we became the team everyone loved to hate. I probably looked out of place with my reputation as someone who was squeaky clean. Gerald Davies, the former Wales wing who was one of my heroes as a boy and who is now a journalist, wrote that the Neath players looked like a gang of extras in a Sam Peckinpah movie, with their cropped haircuts and fierce expressions, but I felt at home from the day I joined. I suppose there was an element of madness, but as a rugby team Neath took some beating. I wished I had joined them sooner and to leave the club less than two years after arriving was a wrench.

In September 1990 the Welsh Rugby Union had just started a national league, three years after England had gone down the same road, and our first match had been at home to Abertillery. That morning I received a call from a rugby league scout: would I be interested in going to watch Warrington the following day with a view to signing for them? I had had approaches from Castleford and Hull Kingston Rovers in my Maesteg days, but they had not amounted to anything. Rugby league was a sport which held no interest for me; I knew nothing about the game or its players, but something took me to Warrington and the day after I had watched them I had agreed to sign for them.

As a courtship, it was unusually brief. There was none of the prior speculation in the media which usually greeted a union player who was considering turning professional and it was a rare case of the deal being signed and sealed before anyone knew anything about it. It was a decision made for all the wrong reasons; not that my time at Warrington was unfulfilling, but on reflection I would not make it again. I did not tell Mum until the deed was done because I knew what her reaction would be.

'How can you do it?' she asked after I had told her that I was going. 'You have only just broken into the Wales team. You must be mad.' In those days, going from union to league was a one-way ticket: there was no return. I was not to know that union would go open in August 1995, but it was precisely because of the stresses and strains caused by amateurism, the need to hold down a full-time job while juggling the increasingly time-consuming demands of rugby as well as family commitments, that I and others went north.

A newspaper said that I went because Neath would not provide me with a sponsored car. This came from a flippant remark made off the cuff by me because I could not explain my decision. There was no rational reason for it, but it is not as if things turned out badly for me. It has not quite been Manchester United and Old Trafford, but I would probably have got no further there than cleaning boots. Mother did know best and I showed a clean pair of heels instead.

TWO

SEVENS

They say that the first cut is the deepest, and though my career has taken me a long way from my home in Caerau, I have always looked out for Maesteg's results. Never the most fashionable of clubs, they have declined in recent years and are no longer in the top two divisions of the league in Wales. Known as the 'Old Parish', Maesteg was where I cut my rugby teeth and the club provided the foundation for my future success.

I very nearly did not make it with Maesteg. I came out of youth rugby thinking I would make the step up to the senior team immediately. I had won three Welsh Youth caps in the centre, in the same squad as Mike Rayer, Nigel Davies and Greg Prosser (who were all to be capped by Wales at senior level) and Dean Conway, who is currently the England cricket team's physiotherapist. We played South African Schools in January 1984 at Stradey Park in Llanelli, narrowly losing 9–6 after anti-apartheid protestors had staged a demonstration outside the ground before the kick-off. I had had an invitation to train with Neath whose coach, Ron Waldron, was then part of the Welsh Youth set-up. I had played two matches for Maesteg at the end of the 1983–4 season, making my debut against Cross Keys in a match I have always thought we lost. Research shows that we won 21–10. My rugby recall is not the best. I have always been someone who lives for today; yesterday is gone and it holds little in the way of relevance. I have not collected much in the way of memorabilia or mementoes from my career which I may come to regret in later years, but looking back is not my style – unless a bigger and faster opponent is making ground on me.

I had a trial with Maesteg in the summer of 1984 and, drunk on the innocence of youth, I assumed a place in their squad was mine. Instead, I was told 'thanks but no thanks'. It was the end of August and I had turned Neath down, having previously declined an offer to go with Bridgend on a summer tour because of what I felt was a dutiful loyalty to my home town club. I was a rugby player without a team. I ended up going to a local side, Maesteg Celtic, to ask if there was a game going. I had a telephone call one Saturday morning: the 3rd XV needed a centre and I had to get down to the club quickly. The big time beckoned.

I arrived, boots and all, only for fate to lend a hand. The first team were due to leave for their match in Senghenydd and they needed a centre. I stayed in the team for the rest of the season, playing five matches for Maesteg on permit at the end of it. Looking back now, I have no recollection of the matches I played for Celtic but I must have done something because I was voted player of the year. It was very much social rugby, with no payments of any kind, and at that stage I was more concerned with my career off the field. After leaving school with two A levels in Maths and Biology, I studied medical laboratory sciences at Neath Tertiary College and ended up taking Fellowship examinations at the then South Glamorgan Institute of Higher Education. This eventually gave me letters after my name: AIMLS – Associate of the Institute of Medical Laboratory Sciences.

I had left school at 18 and it was a time of high unemployment in areas like the Llynfi Valley, of which Maesteg was a part. The staple industries in Wales of coal and steel were being run down and jobs were scarce. I had stayed on at school after taking my O levels because I knew that the more qualifications I had, the better my chances of avoiding the dole queue. Previously, I had gone to Plasnewydd Primary School in Maesteg, rather than Garth School which was closer to my house, because it had rugby on its curriculum. It was then on to Maesteg Comprehensive where I was regarded as a quiet, studious pupil, though I did have my moments. I was virtually reclusive until I reached the age of 11, staying indoors and watching television or playing with the hundreds of toy soldiers I had. I was shy and introverted and I hardly had any outdoor life.

I came out of my shell slightly at the comprehensive, and I did get six of the best with the cane after a prank in a geography class backfired. A group of us were composing saucy messages from the female teacher (whose name I forget) to a member of the class. Mine was intercepted and I had to face the music. I was also asked to leave the school in the first year of sixth form after another escapade involving locking a girl in the toilets, but I did not see leaving as an option because it would have left me with no career to follow and I knuckled down for my final year. My reports were generally good and I acquired a habit for reading; not so much fiction as books on mathematics and science. It was a habit which was to earn me one of my many nicknames during my rugby career. When I was at Richmond, Craig Quinnell, after flicking through something I was reading, decided that it was literature which had zero swap-value and which offered even less in terms of stimulation. 'Boring Book Bateman', my fellow Wales internationals dubbed me.

My rebellious streak as a teenager was confined to a few months when I did not have a haircut. A friend and I, a bit late for the hippie revolution and flower power, decided to hitchhike our way to Donnington where there was a rock festival. We had got as far as the Severn Bridge and were walking along the M4 when we heard the sound of sirens. A police car pulled up, someone yelled 'Oi you!' and we were off over the nearest hedge and across a field. We looked behind us and saw two rather overweight policemen struggling to keep up. We could easily have lost them, but we did not have a clue where we were running to and decided the best course of action was to let them take us in. Perhaps we would end up further along the M4.

We were taken to a police station in Bristol and strip-searched. Given the look of us, all denim and uncut hair, the law had decided that we must have been carrying drugs. After nothing was found, we were told we could go. We asked for a lift to the M4, only to be informed that it was no place for hitchhikers. We decided to make our own way there only for someone to stop and take us to Donnington before we had another chance to break the law. The journey proved more memorable than the festival in which the leading acts were AC/DC and Whitesnake. I have not been hitchhiking on the M4 since.

My year in junior rugby was far from a waste. Someone at Maesteg had told me that it would be better playing regular rugby than sitting on a bench, but I could not see the value in stepping down a grade at the time and I still think it was the wrong advice. When I joined Maesteg the following season, I was able to command a regular place. I was not the biggest of centres and the year with Celtic had hardened me up physically. It was still a step up in terms of pace and physique, and in those days Maesteg were able to hold their own in the old Whitbread Merit Table, an invitation 'league' in which sides were not obliged to play each other. The champions were awarded a pennant, but it did not really mean anything and there were seasons when clubs in with a chance of finishing top would hastily arrange fixtures against sides near the bottom in order to raise their percentage. As a player, you wondered why there was not an official league, but rugby union was amateur then in far more than just name. The word 'league' conjured up notions of professionalism and a threat to the very fabric of the sport, but once the World Cup was introduced in 1987, the beginning of the end had started for the old guard.

Not that amateurism meant not getting paid. When I joined Maesteg, they paid the princely sum of one pound for every win. Travelling expenses were paid out at twenty-two pence a mile which meant that, in a good month, I would pocket twelve pounds. You were not in it for the money, but rumours did abound of what clubs elsewhere were paying. Neath were among those suspected of tempting players to the Gnoll by offering them significant inducements, but their win bonus was only five pounds and when we won the Welsh Cup in 1989, we did not receive anything. A year later, after we had held on to the trophy, every player received fifty pounds. There used to be a door in the Neath club through which the players would pass every Thursday evening to receive their brown envelopes. The club was the most successful in Wales, and probably Britain, when I joined, and my monthly 'wage' used to be around forty pounds, a more than tidy sum in those days and a welcome supplement to my wages.

Looking back now, I cannot understand where the money went.

Neath would regularly play to packed houses, with some spectators shinning up the floodlights to get a decent view. There were no turnstiles at the ground and there was never an official attendance figure at a match, merely a figure someone thought of which would always err on the conservative side. Clubs like Neath must have made a considerable sum of money, but only a fraction of it found its way to the players. Not that we complained, but after I had left for Warrington, the struggle for supremacy in the national league, which was introduced in 1990, meant that clubs started throwing more and more cash at players and the strains on amateurism became unsustainable.

I played 136 matches for Maesteg, the most appearances I was to make for a union club, and in those days teams would often arrange more than 50 fixtures a season. Players would frequently pile up more than 500 appearances for a club with Wednesday night games running virtually throughout a season. A litmus test of a player's durability and worthiness used to be whether he could come through 'a wet Wednesday night at Maesteg' and there were times when established internationals decided that there was no need to come to Llynfi Road on a floodlit evening in deep midwinter. Midweek matches are now a rarity and players of yesteryear wonder why their modern counterparts, who may make no more than 25 appearances a year, often complain about fatigue and fixture congestion.

Having seen life from both sides, a big difference today is the amount of training players put in. In the amateur days, you would train on Tuesday and Thursday evenings and very often you played to get and keep fit. Players now put more in in terms of hours than they ever did before, hardly surprising given that the sport now provides us with a living – but it is not a case of one way being better than the other. There is nothing to be gained in looking back, and while it is easy to get nostalgic about the old days, and it was a player's game then in the sense that you did what you wanted without any contractual obligation, rugby union is a far more exciting game to play now. Improved fitness levels have given it an added dynamism and such is the physical nature of the game at the top that it would not be possible to sustain the old programme of two fixtures a week; players would be burned out by the time they were 25.

Back in the 1980s, playing twice a week seemed natural. Despite a proud history and the distinction of being the last first-class Welsh club to go through a season undefeated (as the Old Parish did at the end of the 1940s) Maesteg were not regarded as a fixture secretary's biggest catch, so many of our games against the top clubs were staged on a Wednesday night. It was the perfect time to play the likes of Cardiff, Swansea and Llanelli who rarely arrived with their strongest teams. Saturday was regarded as prime time, but gates were generally better midweek. Supporters of junior clubs, who did not play on Tuesdays or Wednesdays because they did not have floodlights, would turn out then whereas they were elsewhere on weekends. Matches are a sport's main currency and the virtual loss of midweek rugby coincided with a marked downturn in the fortunes of the Welsh game, together with fixture lists which offered far less in terms of variety, with the English clubs involved in their own league from 1987.

As I reflect on my career, Maesteg were without question the most hospitable club I have played for. I had hoped to appear in the centre for them with my brother David. My second trial was his first and, in my view, we outplayed our opponents. But whereas I got the nod, he was turned down and went to a junior club in a neighbouring valley, Nantyffyllon. Maesteg wore dark shirts with a thin yellow band and the club's emblem contained the numbers 7 7 7 7. The Four Sevens could have been the title of a Sherlock Holmes mystery and the story behind the figures has a mysterious feel to it. During the last century, so the legend goes, there was an apprentice stonemason in the Maesteg area whose task it was to chisel out the inscription to someone in the area who had died at the age of 28. The young man was unable to sculpt the figure eight and, working unsupervised, he devised a way round his problem – hence 7 7 7 7.

I had been at Maesteg for 18 months or so when the club's coach, Brian Nicholas, said that he saw me as an international wing and that he wanted me to change positions. The club had a number of promising centres: Stuart Pardoe, Mike Hall (who was to go on to play for Wales) and Andrew Evans. Nicholas was an enigmatic man, a very deep thinker about the game but someone who was very hard to read. Moving to the wing held little appeal for me, but if there was a chance of a cap I thought 'why not'. If I had pondered for a little longer, I would have reflected that Colin Donovan, a Maesteg wing from the end of the 1970s who was a prolific try scorer, had had his international cause championed by many only to finish his career uncapped. I never got the call while I was at Maesteg, and nor did Hall who moved to Bridgend in his quest for fame, followed not long afterwards by Nicholas himself.

Nicholas did a lot for Maesteg. As one of the Wales Youth coaches, he was able to attract youngsters to Llynfi Road but they rarely stayed too long. We finished third in the Merit Table, but when Nicholas cut his ties with the club, it began a gradual descent. He has been one of the best coaches I have played under and without doubt the hardest to understand. Sometimes after a conversation with him you felt drained, as if he were trying to psychoanalyse you all the time. He took defeat very personally, and after one reverse at Penarth, a club which then won precious few matches, he paced around the field shaking his head and, after we had boarded the coach for the trip home, he walked in front of it for nearly a mile before getting on.

Gwyn Evans was capped by Wales, though at full-back rather than the outside-half position he filled at club level. Gwyn became a cult figure in the area, someone who proved that you could make it from Maesteg. He remained loyal to the club, a modest man who would have been out of place in a nest of prima donnas. At the end of one season, Maesteg were invited to take part in a Sevens tournament in Lancashire. It was the perfect time to relax and unwind and not let the rugby get in the way. Gwyn, Leighton O'Connor and myself did our best not to win any of our matches so we could take our bow from the tournament and find some refreshment. Gwyn, though, took things a bit far when, in a style Forrest Gump was later to copy, he crossed the try-line but did not touch the ball down until he had gone a few yards over the dead-ball line. There were certain things you could get away with as amateurs.

Gwyn had been at Maesteg for virtually a decade when I joined. I once told him that I could not imagine playing rugby that long, especially if I was not going to make it as an international player. The sad fact was that Maesteg was a dead-end as far as the road to the National Stadium was concerned. Gwyn had proved to be an exception and it was a case of refining my skills, working on areas like passing which needed a lot of attention. I have always been fortunate that I have been quick off the mark, even as I left my mid-30s behind, and I could understand why Nicholas wanted to try me out on the wing: I was not the biggest of centres, weighing in at 13 st and standing at less than 6 ft, but it was not the place for me.

I had a few matches on the wing but found it too lonely a position. At centre, you were far more involved. There is nothing worse on a cold, wet day than standing around waiting for the ball to come to you. In those days, wings were not encouraged to come infield looking for the ball and if it was a match when the forwards decided to stick the ball up their collective jumper and not let anyone else play with it, you had more of a chance of catching a cold than the ball. I told Nicholas that my days as a wing were over, diplomatically saying it was because I felt I was not quick enough, and he agreed to only consider me as a centre. The very next game we were at Swansea. I had been chosen in the midfield only for one of the wings, Wayne Thomas, to fail to show up. 'Just do it one more time,' pleaded Nicholas. It was not only me who cursed Wayne's absence. The Swansea wing Arthur Emyr had been chosen to play for Wales the following week, but he never made it. I pinned him in a tackle and his ankle went. It marked an unusual family double for me: the previous Wednesday, Maesteg had played Penarth. Arthur's brother, Dafydd, was in their team and he also failed to see the match out after I hit him hard in a tackle and he broke his ribs.

Many years later, at the end of the 1990s, I was chosen to play on the wing by Wales. Their new coach, Graham Henry, had been in the country for less than a year. He was surprised at my reaction to the selection. I told reporters that I hated playing on the wing and that I was a centre, pretty much full-stop. The remark inspired large headlines and Graham was less than amused. I had not intended to imply that I would rather not have been picked. All I was saying was that my previous outings on the wing had been unhappy ones. As it turned out, the nature of the position had changed so much that my fears of being detached from the game turned out to be unfounded and at that stage of my career (I was 34) I was not going to go on about a lack of pace.

I do not think that I could have had a better start to my career than at Maesteg and when I moved to Neath at the beginning of 1989, I did not do so because I thought I stood a better chance of winning a Wales cap from the Gnoll. Using the experience of Gwyn Evans as an example, I convinced myself that being overlooked by Wales had nothing to do with the club I was playing for and everything to do with me as a player. I was not good enough to cut it at the top level and, while I generally got good reviews in the media, it was my contemporaries, Mike Hall, John Devereux and Nigel Davies, who went on to bigger and better things.

I thought about packing in the game. If I was not up to playing for Wales, what was the point in trying to hold down what was in effect an unpaid second job? Nicola, my wife, persuaded me to carry on, pointing out that there was more to rugby than Wales. Maesteg was very much a family club with a strong sense of community. The players were a close-knit group and we regularly stayed behind in the clubhouse after matches, singing the diehards there into submission. I saw a lot of the world thanks to Maesteg, playing Sevens in Dubai and Monte Carlo for Crawshay's Welsh and travelling to Italy with Glamorgan. I played for West Wales at Under-23 level and in 1987–8, I was voted Maesteg's player of the year.

Neath renewed contact with me through one of their wings, Alan Edmunds, who had been in the Dubai Sevens with me. Ron Waldron, their coach, and Brian Thomas, the club's manager, visited me at work in Morriston Hospital. 'If you want to play for Neath, you have got to want to play for Neath,' said Thomas. He had been instrumental in pushing through a revolution at the club a few years earlier which effectively ended the traditional committee system and replaced it with a management team, with shades of what was to come much later under professionalism. I dithered: the Maesteg coach Duncan Rees, who had taken over from Nicholas, tried to persuade me to stay, saying I was a local lad who would never feel at home elsewhere. The reason why I had joined Maesteg in the first place, rather than Bridgend or Neath, was out of a sense of duty but halfway through the 1988–9 season I decided that my first duty was to myself.

My last game for Maesteg, at the start of the new year, was against Neath. The lure for me was not so much that I felt I had a better chance of being capped from Neath (I still naïvely believed that ability counted for far more than who you played for) but because they were playing New Zealand that autumn and I thought it would be my one chance to face the All Blacks. As it turned out, I was playing for Wales within 14 months and without doubt that had as much to do with where I was playing as with my ability because by then Waldron had taken over as the Wales coach. It was a case of being in the right place at the right time.

THREE

HOUSE OF GAIN

'Welcome to the House of Pain' is the sign which should have been nailed on to the door of the visitors' dressing-room at the Gnoll at the end of the 1980s. This was a ground where everyone feared to tread and these were heady days when Neath scored tries for fun and broke records galore. Despite their success at club level, they were not over-represented in the Wales side and that created a sense of injustice which was reflected in the way we played: no prisoners and no mercy. When the inevitable happened and Wales turned to Neath after a run of poor results and made Ron Waldron their third coach in two years, the bubble burst. By then, I was with Warrington and the way the Wales tour of Australia in 1991 collapsed so ignominiously on and off the field was taken as proof that the Neath way had nothing to commend it at international level. But I do not accept that. The problem to me was that the other clubs in Wales had not seen how the game was changing and how attention needed to be paid to details like fitness and a fluid gameplan. Ron was ahead of his time and, in the light of what has happened since, it is time that his reputation was restored.

I turned up for my first training session at Neath without my kit, which turned out to be a good way of breaking the ice. It was not a club where a red mat greeted your arrival and the players there said that they thought Ron had been more interested in another centre at Maesteg. There was an insularity about Neath and they felt that, not being part of the rugby establishment, they were battling against the world. Their grievance acted as a stimulus. There was something compelling about the club and I spent 18 of the most fulfilling months of my career there. The supporters took to me immediately and my arrival was timely because Neath had just suffered a rare defeat, against Newbridge, and I was given a place in the side straight away.

I knew Ron from my time with Wales Youth. He had been capped by Wales as a prop in the 1960s, but he was not obsessed with set-piece play. He looked at the way the game was developing in the southern hemisphere and realised that players had to be multi-dimensional. Numbers on the back of jerseys were there more for identification purposes than to denote positions. He wanted props and second rows who could run and handle as well as win ball, and backs who would ruck and maul as well as make breaks: the total team. Neath swept all before them because we had the edge on virtually every side in terms of fitness and in my second season with the club we scored 345 tries, regarded then as a world record. We did not so much beat opponents as overrun them and scores in the 50s, 60s and 70s were commonplace.

It was only natural that Wales turned to Ron halfway through the 1990 Five Nations season. The national scene had been in turmoil ever since the tour of New Zealand in 1988. Tony Gray had gone there as the European coach of the year after guiding Wales to their first Triple Crown for nine years only to be sacked on his return home. John Ryan, who had coached Newport and Cardiff in the 1970s and '80s, took over but the slide continued. The month before I left Maesteg, Wales had played Romania at the National Stadium in Cardiff without a single Neath player in their starting line-up and the subsequent defeat was greeted with virtual euphoria at the Gnoll. Only five Neath players were chosen in a 35-man squad for a training camp in Valencia that January, and in the summer, when Wales B toured Canada in the same summer that the Lions went to Australia, again only five Neath players went.

Welsh rugby is divided up on tribal lines, east against west. Ryan had no support west of Bridgend and as Wales continued to lose, so the knives were sharpened. I had hoped to be in the frame for the tour to Canada, but even with John Devereux and Mike Hall in Australia, I was left in the wilderness. I am not sure whether I was in contention in those days; the only journalist who kept pushing my name forward was Gareth Roberts of the *South Wales Evening Post* (and subsequently *Wales on Sunday*), and it was not until the following season, after Neath had played New Zealand, that I made the breakthrough. The All Blacks beat us 26–15, but at one stage in the second half we were within a point of them after Alan Edmunds scored a well-worked try. New Zealand were then not only the world champions but they were at the height of their powers, unbeaten at Test level for three years and they would go on to beat Wales with a lot more comfort than they had dealt with both Neath and Llanelli. To Ron, the fixture offered the chance to show that the Neath way was the direction Wales should be taking and though the lap of honour we performed after the match might have been slightly excessive given the fact we had lost, it was an instinctive reaction after a performance which should have lifted some of the gloom which had hung over Welsh rugby for what seemed too long.

I think it put pressure on Ryan especially, as Wales lost a one-sided international with New Zealand at the National Stadium by a then record score at home, 34–9. He started to turn more to Neath and I was one of seven players from the club chosen in the Wales squad for the B international against France in Arcachon in November 1989. I ended up partnering Adrian Davies (the young Neath outside-half who was studying at Cambridge University) in the centre. We ended up being overpowered at forward and finished well beaten, 28–15, but it was my first experience of rugby at a higher level. Of the side that took the field that day, only three of us – the full-back Mike Rayer, the flanker David Bryant and myself – reached ten full caps for Wales. Six never made it at all. In those days, France provided the only meaningful B fixture for Wales and to be chosen in the side was a firm indication that the national selectors were interested in you. They were not interested enough in my case, though, because when the squad for the Five Nations Championship was announced the following month, I was not among the 26 players named. Even though John Devereux had joined Widnes shortly after returning from the Lions tour, I lost out to Mike Hall, Ceri Jones, Nigel Davies and David Evans. Ryan, ahead of his time perhaps, had an obsession with size and playing players out of position, though his attempts to turn Hall into a wing and Evans into a centre were not successful.

Ryan placed more emphasis on defence than attack, hardly surprising given that he was trying to stop a poor run of results, but the Welsh squad ended up divided between the Neath players who felt they had seen the future and the players from more fashionable clubs who had their feet under the table and felt comfortable. Ryan's reign came to an end two matches into the championship campaign. A home defeat to France was followed by a then record 34–6 defeat against England at Twickenham, a result which was so humiliating (even if it would not raise eyebrows today) that Ryan immediately offered his resignation. No sooner had it been accepted than Ron was trotted out as his successor. We lost to England on the Saturday and Ron was appointed the following Monday – a move that was far too hasty in the eyes of many who felt that Ryan's position must have been undermined long before he walked the plank. Consequently, as Ron tried to hit the ground running, he found himself in the quicksand of Welsh rugby politics and almost immediately he had that sinking feeling.

By the time of his departure, some 18 months later, after the dismal tour to Australia, his reputation lay in tatters and he needed hospital treatment for a heart complaint. He made a comeback with Neath and dropped down a division with Bonymaen, but it was never the same for him. Everything he believed in and the style of play he so passionately advocated was widely held to be discredited, but I think Ron largely had it pretty right. When he took up the Wales post (which no one should forget was an honorary one in those days) he immediately turned to Neath and I was one of the fortunate ones called up for the international against Scotland at the National Stadium.

I was one of three Neath players called into the team, along with the props Brian Willams and Jeremy Pugh. The scrum-half Chris Bridges was named among the replacements. Scotland had won their opening two matches against Ireland and France and victory against us would set them up for a potential Grand Slam decider against England at Murrayfield. We were looking to avoid the shame of becoming the first Wales side to suffer a Five Nations whitewash. My delight at being called up by Wales was tempered by my fear that it would be seen as a cheap cap, earned because I was playing for Neath rather than because I was good enough to justify my selection. I had the evidence that I had, albeit briefly, figured under Ryan and I had faith in my own ability, but it was clear that Ron and Neath were on trial and we were not going to be given much time to present our evidence. Just as Ryan was undermined by the geographical divide in Welsh rugby, so would Ron be, and this time the boot was on the other foot.

The Scotland game passed in a blur. I remember thinking that the atmosphere had been better on the previous occasion I had played at the ground, the Welsh Cup final between Neath and Llanelli in May 1989 – more 'Welsh' somehow. I gave the scoring pass to the wing Arthur Emyr for our try and I was penalised for deliberately knocking the ball on under our posts. Neath were used to playing a quick game, but this was a pace above anything I had experienced. Scotland's back row of John Jeffrey, Derek White and Finlay Calder, who had all been with the Lions in 1989, dominated the game. They were quick to get to the breakdown and to either kill the ball or make it available, and we lost 13–9 to, as it turned out, the eventual champions. We had not played badly, and in terms of endeavour and shape it was a lot better than what had been served up at Twickenham. But it was also clear that Wales were lagging behind at international level. What we needed was a wider embracing of Ron's ideas. Instead though, after we had lost 14–8 against Ireland in Dublin in a match which was as dreadful to play in as it must have been to watch, any lingering trace of goodwill evaporated.

I was not plagued by nerves before my Wales debut, but the longer my career has gone on, the more I worry before a match: am I getting too old? Will I be letting others and myself down? The concept of age does make me nervous: one poor performance and you will be accused of being past it. When Northampton played Rotherham in the 2000–01 season, I was rooming with Paul Grayson. He asked me if I was looking forward to the match and I said no, I was too nervous.

Paul had played for England at outside-half and he asked me why I did not retire if I was not enjoying myself. We talked for hours and ever since then, when I have suffered an attack of nerves I tell myself to go out and enjoy the 80 minutes and that does calm me. My jitters are nothing compared to those of the Wales outside-half Neil Jenkins, who is regularly sick before matches. How he got on to the field with the Lions in South Africa was a mystery. He had a deathly pallor in the dressing-room, looking more like a hospital case than a match-winner. He and I have taken to talking to each other before internationals but he still goes as white as a sheet as the kick-off beckons.

Nerves did not blight my days with Neath. We hardly lost a match when I was there and won two cup finals. The first, against Llanelli, was a memorable match. They had beaten us in the final the previous year against all the odds and we were ready for them. Then in 1990, we defeated Bridgend in a sub-standard game when we did not live up to our potential and we were fortunate that Aled Williams missed a number of goal-kicks. From being a club which prided itself on being anti-establishment, we had turned into the ruling party in the sense that we dominated the Welsh squad and the change in emphasis proved profound.

Neath in those days had a reputation for being an unruly, undisciplined club and the way the Wales squad fell apart in Ron's final days was taken as evidence of that. The truth was different: there was an unruly element and fights between the forwards often broke out in training sessions with players trading punches. Ron would stand in the shadows smiling and he encouraged the competitive element. Things did sometimes get out of hand and some games in the coach on the way back from matches were banned. One was the Parachute Jump where you had to climb on top of seats on either side of the aisle and hurl yourself to the floor to land as flat as possible. Another involved having to slap a player . . . if you were deemed to have hit him too softly, you were slapped by every other player and there were times when guys came off the bus virtually concussed. And then there were the initiation ceremonies which every player new to the club had to go through. I had to wait a month for mine. It came as we journeyed back from London after the Twickenham international between England and Wales. We had played Wasps on the Friday night and stayed in London for the match. On the coach trip back, I was locked in the toilet for about an hour. Every time I tried to open the door, I was set upon and had to lock myself back inside. I had the last laugh, though, because all the cans of beer were stored in the toilet and this bargaining chip eventually got me out in one piece. I was more fortunate than most and there were some players, most notably the second row Paul Jackson, who would take things too far.

As a player Paul had it all but he had a self-destruct button and did not know when to stop. The wing Chris Higgs left Neath because of Paul, who had no respect for authority. He eventually went too far and ended up moving clubs. He had been tipped as a potential Wales international, but he did not have enough self-discipline to make the step up. I never had a problem with him, but there were many in the club who were wary of him.

Training at Neath was hard, with five-mile runs a regular ordeal. Ron felt that we could never be too fit and we were the first club in Wales to appoint a fitness coach. His methods were not widely embraced by some in the Wales squad and there were players who blamed Ron in an attempt to hide their own failings. I would not argue that Ron was the best tactical coach around, but he was the most committed and he knew where he wanted to go. He was appalled at the way some of the top clubs conditioned their squads. He expected players to be fit and when he found they were not he had to spend time putting it right, which left him short when it came to preparing the side tactically. With Welsh rugby so badly divided when he took over and with players not willing or not able to put in the extra amount of work required, he had little chance of succeeding, but many of his ideas came to be embraced by coaches all over the world. Ron lacked the necessary resources and with the 1991 World Cup due to be staged in Britain, he also lacked time. He was hounded into retirement and deserved far better than the condemnatory headlines which greeted his departure as if his failure was a cause for national celebration.

There was no real attempt to look at the reasons behind Wales's decline. When Ron was asked to take over from Ryan, it was as if he were a magician with a magic wand: one wave and everything would be fine. He was forced to turn to Neath players because we understood him, but in the end it became a case of Neath against the rest, because he was forced to call on too many of us and the tensions within the squad meant there was only going to be one outcome. Ron, like Ryan, had not been helped by the loss of players to rugby league. David Young and John Devereux joined the exodus in the 1989–90 season, following players like Jonathan Davies, Adrian Hadley and Paul Moriarty, and in the autumn of 1990 three Neath players turned professional: Rowland Phillips, Mark Jones and myself. Money was only part of the reason for this exodus and in many cases the urge to go was because there seemed no end to the spiral of descent in Wales.

I scored 22 tries in my first, and only, full season for Neath, the most I have managed in a single campaign. Many of them were simple run-ins as we created overlap after overlap, but it was exhilarating to be a part of that side. It was the most enjoyable season of my career, not just because I won my first Wales cap but because we were playing the game as it should be played with everybody involved: 1,900 points and 345 tries told their own story. Being with the club also gave me the chance to achieve my ambition of learning Welsh. I tried to speak to the farming front-rowers Brian Williams and Kevin Phillips in their native tongue. It was easier than trying to talk to them in English. Mark Jones and Alan Edmunds were the life and soul of the club. Had we been Cardiff or Llanelli – fashionable clubs which had the seal of Welsh Rugby Union approval – perhaps the Neath revolution would have had more chance of impacting on the international scene, but many saw us as upstarts and Ron never had the clout he needed.

The 1990–91 season saw the introduction of the national league in Wales, some 15 years after it had first been mooted. Clubs, jealously guarding their right to arrange their own fixtures, held out against the idea but once the game in England had taken the league route it was inevitable that we would follow. A young centre, Scott Gibbs, joined us that season and great things were expected of him. Our first match together was in a friendly at Moseley. After just two minutes, I got a knee in the face and wandered round in a daze before being led from the field with concussion. I thought I was having an epileptic fit and I ended up out of action for three weeks. The next game was our league opener at home to Abertillery. Scott and I lined up in the midfield again, but it was to be more than six years before we appeared in the same rugby union team together – though he was to take my place in the Wales team in the 1991 championship at the tender age of 19. I had received a telephone call out of the blue that morning of the league opener asking if I would be interested in going to see Warrington play the following day with a view to signing for them. Without really thinking about it, I said yes.

Despite having had two approaches from rugby league clubs before, I had never thought about switching codes and to this day I am not really sure why I said yes to Warrington. It was a hasty decision, even if I was struggling to balance the demands of rugby, work and family life. The pressures on international players were becoming intolerable at the start of the 1990s and Ron's response to what he saw as the deficiencies in the Wales squad was to call for more and more training sessions. I was effectively working 80-hour weeks and though I enjoyed my job at Morriston Hospital, I was having to ask work colleagues for more and more favours. It did not seem right that while Wales played before sell-out crowds of 52,000 at the National Stadium with gate takings alone topping a million pounds, the players received nothing. After we had beaten Llanelli in the 1989 Welsh Cup final, the WRU did not even lay any food on for the players after the match (the following year they splashed out for some ham and chips). We went quickly back to the Gnoll afterwards, where there was a carnival atmosphere and plenty to eat and drink. Warrington caught me at a vulnerable time, but despite everything I should have stayed put.

In the summer of 1990, I was on my first Wales tour. Namibia was hardly the most exotic location: I played in the two Tests there, partnering Mark Ring in the centre, a Jack-the-Lad figure who played for Cardiff and who was regularly clashing with Ron. Ring had such a natural talent with a gift for the unexpected that there was no way Ron could drop him, but Ringo's capacity to infuriate knew no bounds and he would constantly wind Ron up. The Tests were both close with Namibia at that stage looking to break into the top 15 countries in the world. We won the first 18–9, helped by the sending off of their full-back Andre Stoop for an outrageous head-butt on our wing Steve Ford; and the second 34–30. We ended the six-match tour with a 100 per cent record. Ireland went to Namibia the following summer and lost both their Tests.

I took unpaid leave to go on the tour. The hospital said they would pay me for the month away, but again that would have been loading more work on to others and I suggested that they hire a locum. Ron used the tour to get his fitness methods over to the non-Neath players, though it was a Neath forward, the prop Jeremy Pugh, who ended up running less than most, often pulling out of the cross-country runs with jogger's nipple. We had a £60-a-week tour allowance but most of that was blown on telephone calls. We effectively paid for the privilege of playing for our country, but we never really questioned it and such was our determination to get into the international side that nothing else really mattered. I got to know Ron well in Namibia and it was clear talking to him that I had a long international career ahead of me as far as he was concerned.

Namibia was a country which was looking to catch up with the modern world. We went to one place which was full of swastikas and German war memorabilia; very South African in that sense. Cities were hundreds of miles apart and we seemed to spend half our time on a coach travelling along roads which were not exactly the standard of the M4. Both the internationals were played in the capital, Windhoek, and the behaviour of the crowd was disgraceful. Oranges and cans were thrown at us and Stoop's dismissal for the head-butt only served to increase their indignation. The Englishman Fred Howard took charge of both the internationals and he said they were the quickest games he had ever taken charge of – a sign that Ron's message was starting to get through. Six Neath players were in the side for the first Test and Kevin Phillips was the captain. There was no rift within the squad. It was a hard tour because there was no nightlife to speak of and we were confined to barracks most of the time. We were told not to go out on our own and we were only allowed a beer if we had played a match. Everything was regimented and inflexible, but we were not out there on holiday. The pity for Ron was that his next tour saw Wales go to the country which had by then established themselves as the best in the world, Australia. I had joined Warrington and was into mushy peas by then.

FOUR

BEWILDERED OF WILDERSPOOL

One minute I was looking forward to a league campaign with Neath and Wales's first meeting with the Barbarians and the next I was playing a game which was completely foreign to me, trying desperately to come to terms with alien concepts, such as not playing the ball in the tackle. It was a wet Friday night in Warrington and I was wondering what I had done and how I could have turned my life upside down in less than a week.

After I signed, I spoke to some journalists to explain why and I mentioned the fact that players at Neath did not have sponsored cars. It was just something to say, but a headline the following day suggested that I would have stayed at Neath had they given me a car! It was not true. The problem was to do with the conflicting demands between work and rugby: I could not afford to give up my job at Morriston Hospital but unless I put in the increased time which Ron Waldron was demanding, I could see myself falling out of the international reckoning. I was trying to burn the candle at both ends and it was a struggle. But even that did not really tell the true story; the truth was that there wasn't one. I left Neath for Warrington for reasons I still cannot explain. Opportunity presented itself and I did not take the time to weigh up my options properly. The fact that Kevin Ellis, a close friend of mine, had signed for Warrington the previous May, had some influence and I knew that the Neath and Wales flanker Rowland Phillips was about to join them. Even though

I'd had five successful years at Wilderspool which provided the platform for my move to Australia with Cronulla in 1995, I made the wrong decision. I should have stayed at Neath. I am not normally an impulsive person, but this was an instance when I acted without engaging my brain properly. When I was at Maesteg, Hull Kingston Rovers asked me to come and visit the club. I did arrange a time, but pulled out of the meeting.

Things happened at bewildering speed in 1990. I was getting ready for the Abertillery game when the telephone rang. Les Miles, who acted as a rugby league scout in South Wales, wanted to know if I would be free to travel with him to Warrington the following day. The club had expressed an interest in me to him and he was following it up. The Warrington coach Brian Johnson had watched the 1990 Welsh Cup final between Neath and Bridgend and I had caught his eye. He had been looking at the Bridgend scrum-half Kevin Ellis, a close friend of mine, who signed for Warrington that summer, and when Johnson found himself short of a centre after the start of the rugby league season, he remembered me and asked Les to establish contact.

Les drove me up and back in a day. Warrington lost by 40 points to Leeds in the first game of rugby league I had ever watched and my abiding memory of the match was the way John Gallagher, the former New Zealand full-back who was rated the best player in the world in his position before he turned professional, got forcefully hit time and again. I spoke to Johnson in the clubhouse after the match and the scene was almost surreal. He stood in a track-suit, chewing gum, surrounded by kids who were clamouring for autographs. He looked me up and down, muttered a few words and then produced a crumpled scrap of paper. 'Take it or leave it,' he said, handing it to me without looking at it before turning his attention back to the gaggle of young admirers. And that was it. No pleasantries or prolonged courtship, no inquiry about what I had thought of the match or the club.

I stole into the Gents to see what had been written down: £100,000 over five years with a car thrown in and a house paid for for the first 12 months. I made up my mind there and then to go for it, though had I stopped to think I would have realised that the sum was less than Nicola's (who worked at the Sony factory in Bridgend) and my combined salaries at that time. I told Les in the car going back to Wales that I would be interested if Warrington paid my tax and national insurance over the five years. He rang me at work the following day to say that that was acceptable and I called Nicola who said I should do what I thought was right. And that was it – I was a Warrington player little more than 48 hours after I had originally been approached. There had been no media speculation and Neath were totally unaware of what was going on. I rang Ron Waldron and the team manager David Shaw on the Monday night to tell them that I was going north. They both wished me luck and neither expressed any surprise; nor did they try to persuade me not to make the move, which surprised me. Had I encountered some resistance, I may have been persuaded to stay but so many players had left the Welsh game for rugby league since the 1987 World Cup that there was little officials involved in the union game felt they could do.

I officially signed for Warrington on the Wednesday and two days later I was making my debut for the A side. I found myself playing a game I knew nothing about and had the same amount of interest in. A number of Welsh players were given a tough time on their arrival north, usually because they had received a lot of attention and were well-known names. Allan Bateman hardly rang any bells up north and if every player in the club had been shown my photograph, Kevin apart, I doubt that anyone would have recognised it. That worked to my advantage because I did not have to run a gauntlet of resentment on my arrival. No one ever bad-mouthed me in training and no opponent ever suggested, in basic language, that I 'take myself back to Wales'. The transition from amateur to professional was as smooth as I could have wished for, but I still felt like an outsider in a foreign land.

Leaving Neath had not presented a problem contractually because I was an amateur, but when I left Morriston Hospital I was meant to serve out a month's notice. My boss, Ken Bond, could not believe it when I told him what I had decided. He recovered quickly though and was superb to me. He told me to get up to Warrington and that he would sort out everything with the hospital. He also said that there would be a job waiting for me should I ever come back. Ken retired in 2000 and I went to his leaving do. Coming back to Neath in the summer of 2001, I wondered if the invitation still stood. I had enjoyed my job there. I worked in the pathology department which earned me the nickname 'Quincy' at Neath, but it did not involve cutting up dead bodies and determining the causes of death. My field was haematology and my role was varied: cross-matching blood for accident victims; blood counts; dealing with burst arteries. I could be called out nine or ten times a night. The job meant I had to be available for 24 hours a day, twice a week and there were weeks when I put in 80 or 90 hours. It got to the point when I constantly needed my colleagues to swap shifts because of my rugby commitments and I was embarrassed to ask them.

I thought that joining Warrington would mean an end to my dual occupation, but within a few months I was looking for a part-time job in a hospital or clinic. I found I had a lot of time on my hands and most of the other players at the club had other jobs. Pay levels were low and a number of players were on less than ten thousand pounds a year. Small wonder, then, that hostility was felt towards players from Wales who had never played the game but were able to command big signing-on fees and hefty wage packets. We were seen as taking bread from the mouths of those who had been part of rugby league all their lives and it was hard to argue with that. I could not see then, and I still cannot now, why it was that so many league clubs signed union players knowing that the chances were that they would not succeed. There were exceptions, like Maurice Richards, David Watkins, Frank Wilson and Jonathan Davies, but there were more zeroes than heroes. It was easy to see why as I turned up for my first training session at Warrington. Rowland Phillips had signed with me and we spent the time practising rolling the ball under our feet after a tackle. The following day was the A match against Halifax and despite the best efforts of Clive Griffiths, the Welshman who was on the coaching staff at Warrington, I was just not prepared for what was to come and for Rowland, a forward, the adjustment from rugby union was to prove even more difficult.

I was more nervous than I ever had been in my life on the day of the Halifax A match. I asked myself what was happening and what I was doing there when I could have been looking forward to Neath's second league match. Rowland's family came up to watch the match and I stayed in his house all day. Nicola could not get the time off work. I started off the game on the wing and, though I had been told how quick a game of rugby league was, I thought the way we had played at Neath would see me through comfortably. I remember laughing when I was told that the half-time interval lasted ten minutes compared to the two we made do with in union, but after ten minutes playing against Halifax A I could not wait for the break to come. I was dead on my feet and it was worse for Rowland who, as a forward, was more involved in the game than I was. League requires a different sort of fitness to union: while you tend to cover more ground in the latter, in the former you have to make explosive bursts over 10 or 20 metres. We won comfortably enough though, and a week later I found myself in the centre against Wigan A. I scored a try in our defeat and two days later, I made my first-team debut against Hull. I lasted 20 minutes before twisting my ankle.

My next outing was against the Australian touring side and I found myself in the centre against Mal Meninga and Gene Miles, two midfielders who looked like monsters to me. They beat us 26–9 in a game more physical than I had ever experienced before. I was not overawed, though, by the quality of the opposition and came to enjoy it. I had been confronted with the best in the world that rugby league could offer and I had coped. From that day on, I was far more relaxed about my new career. I was fortunate that I was accepted by my Warrington team-mates almost immediately. Because wages were low, players relied on their win bonuses and the way to earn respect was to be seen to give your everything and not lay yourself open to charges of just taking the money. The respect was not one-way. League was a brutally hard game and one of the Warrington wings, Des Drummond, was in the veteran stage when I joined the club. He had been capped by Great Britain and was recognised as one of the game's best. He ran a pub in Manchester's Moss Side and he was someone who took no messing: we quickly became firm friends.

The first-team matches were on a Sunday and after a game I would get into the car and drive to Wales, punching the air when I passed the sign on the road to Monmouth which read 'Croeso I Cymru'. It took a good year before the yearning to return to my homeland subsided. I regularly returned to Neath, and whereas in the old days rugby union players who had turned professional were shunned by their former clubs, with many being banned from returning to their old stamping grounds, there was none of that nonsense at the Gnoll. I celebrated when Neath won the inaugural Heineken League title, even though my part in the achievement had been a solitary appearance. There was considerable mirth when I turned up in a sponsored car with my name plastered all over it. Warrington also won a trophy that year, defeating Bradford Northern 12–9 in the Regal Trophy final in a dour, hard game. Our win bonus was £1,200, which I compared to the £50 I had received from Neath for winning the Welsh Cup the year before. Kevin Ellis did even better, breaking into the Great Britain squad 11 weeks after turning professional.

In the summer of 1991, Ron's reign as Wales coach came to a sad and premature end after the tour to Australia which set new lows on and off the pitch. Wales had again gone through the Five Nations without a victory (avoiding the whitewash with a draw against Ireland) and a clear split had developed between the Neath players and others from different clubs. The Cardiff contingent, in particular, were unhappy with Ron's training methods and questioned his selection policy. I took no pleasure from Wales's continued decline and I felt partly responsible. With virtually a full team of players up north, it was my view that we had to take our share of responsibility for what had happened. No other country had suffered such a loss of resources and Wales's fall coincided with the rise of England, which made it all the more hard to bear. As a club, Neath were badly scarred by Ron's experience and, though they were to win the league title again in 1996, they no longer inspired fear.

I never expected to make it as a rugby league player, so when I was called into the Great Britain squad in 1992, it meant more to me in terms of achievement than when I was first capped by Wales. I played against France in 1992 and 1993 and I was on the bench in 1994 when Great Britain defeated Australia at Wembley, Jonathan Davies scoring a superb individual try. The week before this match, I had pulled my hamstring in the dying minutes of a nothing game against Doncaster and when I turned up at the first training session for the international, I could hardly walk let alone run. I spoke to Jonathan and he told me to shut up about it and that he would help me get through. Somehow, I managed to get to the day before the match without the coach Ellery Hanley suspecting that anything was wrong. Perhaps it said something about me that no one saw anything unusual in this centre with a limp.

I went to the physiotherapist on the final morning of training and said that I had tweaked my hamstring in the previous day's session. I spent all day on the treatment table and was told that I would be put through my paces the following morning. I was desperate to take my place on the bench, not just because the match was at Wembley, but also because I saw it as a real opportunity to be part of a winning mission against the best team in the world. I needed five local anaesthetics along the length of my hamstring in order to numb the pain and pass the fitness test which amounted to no more than ten-yard sprints back and forth. When I went on to replace Jonathan, who'd fractured his sternum, I could feel the painkillers wearing off. Very quickly I had a chance to go for the line, but I knew that if I tried I would collapse in a heap and discretion triumphed over valour. We received £4,000 each as our win bonus and it was the highlight of my career – until Northampton defeated Munster in the 2000 Heineken European Cup final at Twickenham. We enjoyed a big night-out in London. Shaun Edwards, the scrum-half who was sent off for high-tackling Bradley Clyde, was then going out with Heather Small of M People and we could get in anywhere with our Great Britain blazers.

Warrington were not that successful during my five seasons with them and the only silverware we won was the Regal Trophy in 1991 when we finished ninth in the league. We finished joint top in 1993–4 along with Wigan and Bradford but we ended up third on points difference. We made the Regal Trophy final again that season but lost to Wigan and in 1994–5 we were fourth. Jonathan had joined us by then, but we were not really going anywhere as a club and when the time came for me to discuss terms for a new contract, I was not sure if I wanted to stay. That decision, however, was made for me.

In 1991, Nicola and I celebrated the birth of our daughter, Naomi, but fatherhood was to bring me one of the stranger injuries of my career. The following year, I was giving Naomi a bath when I jarred my back. The problem did not clear up and when I turned up for a match against Workington, I collapsed in a heap on the floor and could not play. I was taken to hospital where I remained for a week, unable to leave my bed apart from the times when I was wheeled to a swimming pool for exercise. My condition was so bad that I had to be winched out at the end of my splashing-about sessions. I took a fair bit of stick from less than sympathetic team-mates.

Naomi's first introduction to rugby came when she was 16 days old and was at a match with Nicola. It was Boxing Day and someone had left a cigarette smouldering in the ladies' toilet underneath the stand at Naughton Park, Widnes, which started a smoke alarm screeching. Memories of the Bradford City fire were still fresh and the stand was evacuated and the kick-off delayed for 20 minutes.

I found training at Warrington a lot easier than it had been at Neath. You were left to your own devices for the most part, trusted to keep yourself in condition. A group of us formed the Wide Awake Club which saw us rise at 6.30 a.m. to go to the gym at the Warrington club and work out on the weights. I would end up returning home and crashing out for a few hours, dragging myself out of bed to go to the evening training sessions at the club not quite so wide awake. I did it for a few months before getting a job. Warrington's conditioning coach was a local bin-man, Phil Chadwick, who had never played a game of rugby league in his life. He was a fitness fanatic whose enthusiasm was infectious. When I joined Richmond in 1996, Clive Griffiths moved just up the road to take charge at London Welsh and he brought Phil with him.

The one sin-binning in my career came during my time at Warrington after obstructing an opponent against Widnes. I also dropped my only goal during my time here – a stunning effort at the end of a game against Sheffield in 1994. We were 20 points ahead and I thought 'why not'. My only previous attempt, during my Neath days, had ended in miserable failure, compounded by the fact that the match was live on television. Some players know instinctively when to kick. The most memorable drop goal I saw was at King's Park in Durban in 1997 when the Lions, 1–0 up against South Africa in a best-of-three series, were pressing for victory in the second Test.

Jeremy Guscott found himself close to the posts and as soon as he received the ball, he sent it between the uprights to secure the victory and the rubber. I was watching from the sidelines and, though I like to think I would have acted the same way as Jerry, I suspect I would have put my head down and gone for the line. Instinct would certainly not have told me to go for the drop.

Overall, I enjoyed my time with Warrington once I had accepted the reality of what I had done by leaving Wales and turning my back on the amateur code. Naïvely, I did not think that the door to rugby union was permanently shut to me, despite the strict rule which banned professionals from having any contact with the sport. I felt that Wales, a country where union was the national sport, had been so badly ravaged by defections north that they would relax the regulations and allow some of us back. We were certainly not treated as lepers by the public, as the Wales rugby league side, which was reformed in 1991, found when we came back to Wales to play internationals at Swansea's Vetch Field and Cardiff's Ninian Park. We played to packed houses and, at a time when Wales were still struggling in union, it seemed that something had to give. I had no idea, as I discussed a new contract with Warrington early in 1995, that the great walls of amateurism were about to come crashing down.

I had signed for Warrington with my eyes closed. I did not have an agent acting for me, and I still do not believe in them, but I did not show the contract to a solicitor either. Good advice would have been to sign for three years with an option for an extra two, but when it came to a new contract I thought that having made it as an international player in league, which had earned me a one-off payment of £4,000, would have enhanced my value with the club. I expected to be offered more than the £20,000 a year (effectively £25,000 when tax and national insurance were taken into account) I had been on since joining and I was reasonably optimistic when I met Johnson and the Warrington chairman Peter Higham.

We met in Peter's house and it was clear from the outset that my bargaining position, and my worth to Warrington, was not quite what I had expected. Peter pointed out that I was 30 and that not many clubs would be chasing a player of that age. They wanted me to become a full-time professional at Wilderspool which would have

ALLAN BATEMAN

meant giving up my job at Acer Environmental, a microbiological consultancy agency in Runcorn. For this sacrifice, they offered me £14,000 a year, cutting my salary by far more than half. I looked at Brian and asked him to explain the logic of the offer. How could they have offered me £20,000 per annum in 1990 when I had never played a game of rugby league in my life and when they had no idea whether I would make it. In contrast, I was now an international player whose ability was not in question. 'Aye,' said Brian, 'but you are not getting any younger.'

I told them that they knew what they could do with their offer; that I would rather give up rugby than my job for that sort of money and I walked out. I suspect they thought I would be back and that now I knew what the local Warrington players had felt when I turned up at the club having signed a six-figure contract. I was a piece of meat whose value had been determined by the fact that I was not likely to go elsewhere and that I could not return to union. As I walked out of Higham's door to get into my car, I thought that my playing days were over. For the second time in my career, I was ready to walk away from rugby but as one door closes, so another opens. My Warrington career was over, but a new beginning was waiting for me Down Under.

FIVE

MR CHIPS, NO PIGEON FANCIER

One of the most commonly used words when talking about rugby union today – and in most sports for that matter – is 'diet'. There are lists of what you should and should not eat. Alcohol is frowned upon and it is like being back at school: 'If you do not eat your pasta, you will not become a big, strong rugby player.' Why is it invariably the case that the things you most like are usually found at the head of the Do Not Consume column? The dietician is the one aspect of the game I will not miss when I eventually retire from playing. The freedom to eat and drink what I want, when I want will be some compensation for the ageing process.

I have been more fortunate than most players because, no matter what I eat, I do not put on weight. I have been allowed the luxury of chips, much to the envy of my team-mates, when on international duty. I even wangled this concession while touring South Africa with the Lions in 1997. I lost four or five pounds in the first couple of weeks there because I could not cope with the pasta which was being rammed down our throats. My body-fat ratio has always been between 8 and 9 per cent, compared to the average of 15 per cent, and when my cholesterol level was tested it also tended to be less than the average. The South Africa tour was one of the highlights of my career, but it also highlighted just why players sometimes grow weary with the demands and rigours of international rugby.

The Lions' fitness coach in South Africa was Dave McLean who made sure that our dietary orders were carried out to the letter. He went around with a little black book, constantly writing notes in it. He had allowed me to order chips as long as no other player saw what I was eating. Others were allowed no latitude. One of the aspects of the tour which I found frustrating was when we would train in the afternoon and then be shipped off to a function before eating. You would stand around drinking a glass of water and making small talk with your stomach turning over as you watched others tucking into the buffet which we were banned from sampling. It was a cruel and dreadful torture with temptation literally put before you on a plate.

It proved too much for the Wales prop David Young at one reception in the British consulate. The nod was finally given for us to get back on to the bus to return to the hotel for something to eat. As we filed out, David picked up a cocktail sausage from a plate and ate it. It was smaller than his little finger and for a man of his size, more than 18 stone, it would have made absolutely no impact, but Dave McLean spotted the indiscretion and duly recorded it in his notebook. The following day, David Young was hauled before the tour committee on a charge of eating a cocktail sausage, found guilty and warned about his future conduct. If it happened again, David was told, the consequences could be serious. He came out of the meeting with a face like thunder and went up to Dave McLean's room but the fitness coach refused to let him in. 'Not while you are in this mood, David!' he shouted through the closed door. It was an absurd incident which did the management no credit.

It was not quite like that when I started my career. When Maesteg made long trips to England, we would have steak and chips for lunch and when I started my career with Wales, steak was the staple diet the night before an international. As dieticians became prevalent in the game, red meat was taken off the menus on the grounds that it lay in your stomach for up to 18 hours and so we carried extra weight during a game. Pasta, which provided energy which you could burn off, came into fashion. Ron Waldron had seen its virtues when he was the coach of Wales. On our 1990 tour to Namibia, he tried to get the players to eat it every day. It was not long before I was making entreaties to Margaret, the wife of the tour manager Clive Rowlands, to order bowls of chips which I would, when Ron was not looking, snaffle. Ron was ahead of his time in stressing the virtues of a diet based on a high carbohydrate intake: rice and pasta for the squad, bread and chips for me. I could not cope with eating food which did not taste of anything.

Alcohol also came to be frowned upon. The average rugby union international is not a teetotaller, but the only over-indulging is done after matches. When I started out with Maesteg, I would regularly have six or seven pints on the night before a match. Nicola's father ran a pub in the town and I would often stay there until midnight when I was the worse for wear and Nicola drove me home. Even when I was at Warrington, there was a period when I would have five or six cans of beer a day. I am fortunate in that I very rarely suffer from hangovers but there was one occasion when, after a Warrington game, I had far too much to drink. The following morning, I had to drive to work in Oldham and was in such a state that I had to pull over on the M56 to be sick. I spent the morning sitting at my desk with my head in my hands.

It was the first time that I had driven while over the limit and I have only done it once since. This was when I was with Richmond. Scott Quinnell, our Welsh number 8, was throwing a New Year's party and other players were there with their wives. I went with Nicola and was feeling sorry for myself because I had broken my nose in the 1997 Boxing Day match against Wasps. My mood had not been improved by a consultant who'd asked me if I was sure that the nose was broken. (As it was splattered all over my face, it did not take much figuring out.) As the party got into full swing, the players threatened to straighten out my nose for me and I grew increasingly agitated. When Nicola refused to give me a New Year's kiss, complaining about my nose, I did not see the joke and stormed out of the house and into my car to drive home – an incredibly stupid thing to do, even if it was out of character.

It was when I had been with Warrington for three years that I gave up drinking alcohol in the week. In 1999, Scott Quinnell and I decided to go on the wagon indefinitely. I lasted for about a month and it did have an effect on my game: an adverse one. Nicola was so concerned about my form that she suggested, to the point of ordering, that I started drinking again. I took her advice and my rugby improved. It may have been coincidence, but every time I am laid up by an injury, I sit it out for three days and then have a few pints. I seem to recover more quickly than I would otherwise.

Drinking before an international is taboo, though in the first few months when Graham Henry took over as Wales coach in 1998 he would bring a crate of beer into the team-room on the Thursday before a match and invite us to help ourselves. Only four or five players bothered, but after we had lost to Scotland and Ireland in the first two matches of the 1999 Five Nations championship, Graham abruptly ended the beer run. Chris Wyatt, the Llanelli second row, was in the Wales squad then and he liked a couple of beers on the night before an international; it helped him relax, but he also smoked and liked to stay up late at night. Each to his own, and to me there should not be a rigid set of rules which are applied to all. As long as you perform in training and in matches, there should be no problem. Graham, though, grew more and more frustrated at not being able to change Chris's lifestyle to the point where he seemed to give up on him after the start of the 2001 championship.

Big matches breed nerves and there are times when players need to unwind. When Wales played Ireland in Dublin in 1998, Leigh Davies was called in to partner me in the centre because Scott Gibbs was injured. Leigh had burst on to the international scene as a 20-year-old in 1996, but the return of Scott and I from rugby league had pushed him back down the ladder. On the Friday night before the Ireland game, the tension was getting to him and Gareth Thomas and I took him out for a drink. We were enjoying a quiet pint when in walked the Wales coach Kevin Bowring and the Welsh Rugby Union's director of rugby, Terry Cobner. I do not think they saw us, and nothing was ever said, but we did not hang around to ask them what they would like to drink. We won the game.

There is a danger of taking things to excess in terms of prohibition. Different players have different personalities but they can get treated like robots. When I was at Northampton, the England squad were made to go for vitamin tests, each paying eighty pounds for the privilege. Hair samples were taken and they had to be of a certain length to provide samples of trace metals and elements. They were told to take certain vitamins if they were found to be lacking in them.

This is taking things way beyond the sport and players were coming to the club armed with tubes of pills, packets and potions. Where is it all going to end? My background is in science, but I often feel that far too much emphasis is placed on diets and fitness regimes and not enough on individual skills. The rugby should come first.

One of the side effects of all this is that players are often scapegoated after a bad performance with critics feeling they do not 'look the part'. It happened to the Quinnell brothers after Wales's 46–12 defeat to England at Twickenham in 2000. We had played poorly in the second half, losing our shape and our discipline, and it was our second successive 34-point reverse at the ground. We took a pounding in the media, which was fair enough, but what I did not expect was some of the personal criticism which came from the England players, summed up by one of my room-mates on the 1997 Lions tour of South Africa, Neil Back, who is without question one of the fittest players around. He took Scott and Craig Quinnell apart, saying effectively that they were a disgrace to their country because they had let their fitness levels slip and were therefore not up to the required standard for an international match.

England had run us ragged in the second half (hardly surprising as we were down to 14 men for 20 minutes with Garin Jenkins and Scott Quinnell both sent to the sin bin) but the writing had been on the wall anyway. England were by far the better team. Neil Back, though, was out of order. Craig had done amazingly well just to take the field. Ever since the World Cup the previous year, he had struggled with a back complaint and the morning after the Twickenham match he could not get out of bed. He went to see a specialist who said that unless he had an operation, not only would his rugby career be at an end but his quality of life would be permanently impaired as well and he would never get a good night's sleep.

Craig and Scott are easy targets because they are naturally big men who only have to look at a plate of chips to put on a few pounds. I know from our time together at Richmond and Wales that they are dedicated professionals. Craig hardly drinks and he sticks rigidly to a diet that would drive me mad. He watches his weight and he trains hard. He is also tremendous company and I just wonder if the brothers are picked on because of their family name. Their father Derek was a Welsh international and a Lion in the 1970s and early 1980s. If they had been a Jones or an Evans, they may have been more anonymous. Scott is one of the best forwards in the world, a player I would have in my team every week and it was a big loss to the Lions when he was forced to return home early in 1997 because of injury.

As characters, the brothers are totally different. Craig is bubbly and extrovert while Scott is more reserved and likes to wrap himself up in family life. When he returned to Llanelli from Richmond in 1998, it was because his wife Nicola wanted to be closer to her family. They were expecting their third child and Scott's departure was keenly felt by Richmond. He did not come cheap to the Scarlets who had to pay a six-figure sum to get him back, but it was money well spent. It was a strange feeling playing for Northampton in the 2000 Heineken Cup semi-final against Llanelli and Scott at the Madejski Stadium, the home of Richmond before the club's untimely collapse. Scott is probably my closest friend in rugby and despite all the criticism he received in the 2000 season (started by former Australia coach Bob Dwyer who described the Quinnell brothers as 'too fat') he has kept his dignity and refused to get involved in slanging matches. I think that it is because of his value to Wales that opponents try to unsettle him by hurling insults, but they are wasting their time. Scott knows that he is respected highly by his colleagues and suggestions that he is unprofessional could not be further from the truth. Craig has been looking to move to Chepstow from Cardiff because people in the city keep on taking verbal pops at him. It is a price of fame, one which the England players rarely have to pay because, as I know from my time at Richmond and Northampton, rugby union there is very much a minority sport, not like it is in Wales.

Despite my penchant for chips and beer, I do look after myself. I have never smoked and it is one habit that I am intolerant of (my grandmother, as I mentioned, used to blow her smoke out of the window in her flat). Rugby players who smoke are doing themselves no favours. The number of smokers is far fewer than it was ten years ago, but I cannot understand why any professional sportsman or woman indulges in the habit which, in the vast majority of cases, will only serve to shorten careers. It's a drag.

Nothing generates publicity like a player who has failed a drugs test. Professionalism means more visits to gymnasiums and weight rooms where, it is commonly assumed, players are tempted by banned substances to take a short cut to bulking up. I have heard many rumours, but I have seen nothing apart from one time when I was at Warrington. Kevin Ellis had been feeling low and someone had given him something to make him feel better. He showed me what he had been told to take: Clembuterol, a drug used to develop muscles in cows. I took them off him and flushed them down the toilet. Kevin had had no idea what he could have been letting himself in for and it could have been the end of his career. In my last two years at Warrington, I was tested for drugs eight times. I regard the taking of banned substances as cheating and, even if I had ever been tempted, I doubt that I would have gone over the top because I hate taking tablets. It took me some time before I finally accepted advice to take aspirin when I had a painful case of shin splints.

These days, you can be tested for drugs anywhere: after a match, at training or even at home. The more often it is done the better as far as I am concerned, though I did not feel that way after Wales had played Italy at Stradey Park in Llanelli at the beginning of 1998. I was badly dehydrated and could not provide a sample. The match had kicked off in the evening and I had to drive back to Richmond that night. I was standing around getting more and more angry and told the guy in charge of the testing that I had had enough and was going home. I invited him to follow me in his car and told him that when I was ready to provide a sample, I would drive into a motorway service station and do the necessary. He said that was not possible and that it had to be done at the ground. I was not taking no for an answer, though, and stormed off to my car. I was about to drive off when Trevor James, the Wales team administrator, banged on my door and begged me to stay. He said that if I went I would be put down as refusing to give a sample. A ban would have been probable and I would always have the stigma of having something to hide. I got out of the car and waited for nature to take its course, arriving back in Richmond in the small hours less than pleased.

Various rumours about drug-taking circulated after the 1997 Lions tour to South Africa, especially when the then England captain

Lawrence Dallaglio was the victim of a kiss-and-tell sting by a London newspaper. He was quoted as saying that recreational drugs had been taken by some of the Lions' players after the series against the Springboks had been won. (He later denied saying this.) I was amazed by the allegations, not just because Dallaglio was one of the last players you would suspect of being caught up in something like that, but because I had not seen any evidence of anything like that on the tour.

One thing that did surprise me was that the South Africans were not heavy on drug-testing and I cannot remember anyone being asked for a sample. There was a heavy emphasis during that tour on players looking after themselves and behaving responsibly, which was driven by the players themselves. Apart from farcical episodes like David Young and that cocktail sausage, we were pretty much left to our own devices. There was no preventing anyone having a beer on the night before a match. It was not encouraged, but it was not outlawed. We were adults and were expected to behave maturely. No one took advantage in a way they may have been tempted to do if there had been a ban on alcohol.

Diets are no fun, but they can lead to humorous incidents. When Wales travelled to Rome to face Italy in 2001, we were put up in a new hotel which was clearly anxious to make an impression. We were given a treat at supper the day before the match: poached salmon on a bed of fancy pasta. The chef had clearly gone to a lot of hard work, but it was chips for me. My bowl was soon emptied – not by me but by the other players, who after sticking their forks into the salmon had virtually been squirted with blood. The poaching had not taken very long and the waiter was summoned. Profuse apologies were offered and we were told we would be treated to another dish. Plates full of meat drizzled with a sauce soon arrived and the players tucked in. Someone made the mistake of asking the waiter what had been served up and the chef soon found himself cooking yet again after the answer had been given: pigeon. I just got on with my second bowl of chips and the others had to wait a while before they were served up with chicken and chips.

When dieticians first came on the scene, certain foods were frowned upon. Ice-cream was one; we were told to eat low-fat yoghurt instead and fizzy drinks were also out. And yet on the night before an international, we were often sent to the cinema to try to help us stay relaxed. Temptation was on offer here in the form of ice-cream, popcorn, hamburgers and various kinds of sugary drinks. It seemed strange to me – you spent the week cloistered in the hotel with your diet carefully scrutinised and you could blow everything at the end of it by eating junk food in the cinema unsupervised. It was not so much that the players were put on trust as the fact that no one had really thought it through. Players should be trusted, and in the 2000–01 season a code of conduct was incorporated into the contracts of the Wales squad players. It was to be enforced not by the management but the players with a sub-committee set up to oversee everything.

The contract was a bulky document which took some reading and it was a long while before the players signed it. When we eventually did so, it was almost with a gun to our heads which made me question its effectiveness in law. We were herded into a room at our hotel in the Vale of Glamorgan before the international against Samoa that November and told not to come out until we had signed. The national contracts changed virtually every year, but this was the first time a formal code of conduct had been included. Some players were worried, but at least it put everything into black and white rather than leaving it to the discretion of the management. And the fact that the code was to be policed by the players meant that if anyone was to be disciplined, it would be at the instigation of his fellow professionals. It was, though, another step away from individuality and towards conformity. Rugby's not only a game any more, it's a living – and it's not the players who are getting fat.

SIX

AUSSIE AL

I have been given enough nicknames in my time to virtually field a team: 'Quincy', because of my occupation off the field; 'Batman', for obvious reasons; 'Boring Book Bateman', a name given to me by Craig Quinnell as he searched my library in vain for a novel by Jilly Cooper or Wilbur Smith ('British Lion, BMW-Driving, Boring Book Bateman' to give it its full, alliterative title) – and 'Shane', my name in Warrington because it was common up north for everyone to call you 'lad' after your name and the constant greetings of 'Hello Allan, lad' conjured up images of the British actor Alan Ladd, the man who played Shane. There was 'The Clamp', because my Wales rugby league team-mates believed I could tackle; 'Golden Bollocks' was used during the days when Kevin Bowring coached Wales because the other players felt I could do no wrong with this coach who many struggled to get on with; I was called 'The Worm That Turned' by Mark Jones when I was at Neath after he found out on the Wales tour of Namibia that I was not the shy, retiring type that he had taken me for; and 'Aussie Al' I picked up during my time with Cronulla Sharks in 1995 and 1996.

The 'Aussie Al' nickname dated from when I was lounging on a beach in Sydney shortly after arriving in Australia. The weather was beautiful and I made the most of it. As I was soaking up the sun, some of my new team-mates went by, wrapped up in jumpers and jackets. They looked at me as if I had arrived from another planet. What I called hot they called cold and I became known as 'Aussie Al' from that moment. My biggest fear when I arrived in Cronulla was that I would not be accepted in what was without any doubt the best rugby league country in the world. I was not quite as apprehensive as I had been after arriving in Warrington, but there was a gnawing fear inside me that I would not be up to it. Again, though, I was fortunate that my arrival was not preceded by my reputation. I was just another Brit hoping to make it.

I had considered the idea of going to Australia for a couple of years, spending a few months there during British rugby league's close season. Nicola and a couple of friends in Warrington made a video compilation of my career with Warrington, Wales and Great Britain. It was a painstaking task and they had to go through hours and hours of footage to make the tape which was sent to an agent in Australia and passed around clubs. I did not think anything would come of it, but almost at the same moment that Warrington were asking me to go full-time and take a pay cut, the chief executive of Cronulla Sharks, Shane Richardson, was trying to get in touch with me. He had watched Warrington play Bradford at Wilderspool, looking at their centre Paul Newlove who I had managed to get the better of. Shane had seen my video, but he did not put two and two together until he got hold of Jonathan Davies to try and coax my telephone number out of him.

Jonathan, not sure what was going down, did not want to put him through to me and eventually the agent David McKnight rang to say that Cronulla were interested in signing me. Jonathan was on his way to Australia having joined the North Queensland Cowboys on an off-season contract. After I had told Warrington that I would rather retire from playing than accept their new contract, I spoke to Shane who said that he was flying over to Britain and I agreed to pick him up at Manchester Airport and take him to his hotel. Rugby league in Australia had just been thrown into turmoil by an attempt to set up a rival organisation to the Australian Rugby League. The new group, Super League, had signed up a number of clubs and players and the ARL were determined to fight back. It was a battle which was to end in the courts after many millions of Australian dollars had been thrown at players. The dispute could not have come at a better time for me personally.

Shane was looking to sign players for the Super League, which Cronulla had agreed to join. All of a sudden, British rugby league players were in demand in Australia: the Great Britain captain Phil Clarke signed for Easts, Jonathan was off to the Cowboys and Kevin Ellis secured a contract Down Under too. Shane asked me what my plans were. I told him that I was retiring from the game because it was not worth my while financially carrying on. He looked at me and handed over a piece of paper. It was an offer from Super League – $165,000 (Australian) for the first year (around £83,000); $175,000 for the second year and a loyalty bonus of $60,000. I would have had to commit myself to Warrington until I was 45 to earn that sort of money. Fortune had smiled on me at the very moment I was about to jump off the cliff. Where, I asked, did I sign?

Shane, as protocol demanded, had to speak to Warrington whose rationale behind their £14,000-a year-offer to me had suddenly been blown apart. Peter Higham asked me not to sign for Cronulla and, during the period that the contract with Super League and Cronulla was being drawn up, Warrington offered to match everything I had been offered, including the loyalty bonus. My word is always my bond, but there is no way I would have gone back to Warrington anyway. They had used me and, in any case, the weather in Sydney promised to be considerably better than it had been in Warrington.

Perhaps Warrington had treated me with disdain because I had negotiated with them on my own. David McKnight was the first agent I had used and he was to be the last. I do not see the point of agents. I am more than capable of setting out my own terms without having to pay someone a hefty percentage to do it for me. I know my worth and what I would be happy with, which is why Warrington so disappointed me. I had not intended to ask for the earth, only for what I felt I merited. Not involving an agent saves a club money, especially when some agents take their fees from clubs rather than players, though it all amounts to the same thing in the end. Why have someone skimming off your cream? Since Cronulla, I have negotiated all my deals myself; none of them have taken long and bargaining positions have not had to be taken up. Other players prefer to hire agents, whether through laziness or because they do not trust their own negotiating skills, but to me they are a waste of time and money.

Signing for Cronulla fulfilled an ambition for me. I knew how to play the game of rugby league, but Australia was the real testing ground and there was a widespread contempt there for Brits. I did worry that I would attract some comments in the dressing-room and on the training field, conscious of the fact that I was dragging my wife and daughter to the other side of the world when I was not sure what lay in store for me – but again I was lucky. I was just a small guy from Wales, a country most of the Cronulla players had never heard of. I grew tired of saying that it was not a part of England, but I think they knew the difference by the end of my time there. I was very popular for the first few weeks. It was a tradition to lay on barbecues to welcome newcomers to the club and these were strange rituals. Little, if anything, was offered in the way of food but there were always copious amounts of alcohol. The training was hard, with far more emphasis on skills than there had been in rugby union or at Warrington, and there were four heavy weight-training sessions a week which I had to attend. The Australians played and trained hard, but they also knew how to relax and it was not long before I felt at home there.

The Cronulla club overlooked Botany Bay and we did some of our pre-season training on dunes which had been used in the film *Gallipoli*. On the top floor of the clubhouse was a Chinese restaurant which could seat 500 diners and there was also a concert hall, a nightclub, other restaurants and a casino in the complex. Cronulla's owner was Peter Gow, Elle McPherson's father, a larger-than-life character. The club had never won any silverware and had gone into liquidation the year before I joined, but it was a far bigger operation than Warrington.

I had signed for Cronulla at the same time as Castleford's New Zealand loose-forward Tawera Nikau. We were meant to fly out to Australia together, but I had to give a month's notice to my employers in Runcorn, Acer Environmental. I could not have taken off immediately anyway because Warrington were still in the play-offs. I ended up making the 26-hour journey on my own; Nicola was also working.

Shane picked me up from the airport and took me to the only hotel in Cronulla, a suburb in the south of Sydney. It was like paradise to me: an array of shops, surf, beaches and bars. I trained with the club the day I arrived. It was pouring with rain, which shattered my illusions somewhat. It was their winter and my one regret today is that I never spent a summer in Sydney. John Lang, who was later to take charge of Australia, was the club's coach. He took me into one of the corporate boxes at the ground and said that the reason I was there was because of the video Nicola and my friends had compiled. Lang said he liked my high work-rate and he immediately made me feel at ease. I knew that what would count was how I performed for Cronulla rather than how I looked on that tape, but at least I could rest assured that I would be judged on merit.

I played my first three games for Cronulla on the wing. The second match was against Jonathan Davies's Cowboys. Wales had just been knocked out of the rugby union World Cup by Ireland in Johannesburg – the second consecutive tournament that they had failed to qualify for the knock-out stage. The Australian media made much of the fact that Jonathan and I were not with our country in its hour of need and if anyone had said then that within 18 months we would both be playing international rugby union again, I would have laughed at them. The world of union seemed a lifetime away and at that stage it appeared that there would be no going back and I did not hanker to do so.

My fourth match for Cronulla was against the Canterbury Bulldogs and I was moved to the centre (much to my delight) but after just five minutes I pulled my hamstring and was forced to hobble off. My replacement, who was none too impressed at having to come on, was Brian Laumatia who had just played the full 80 minutes in the warm-up match between the second teams of both clubs. This was a feature of every match in Australia. When I made my comeback, against Eastern Suburbs, I came on as a replacement after 20 minutes having played the entire 80 minutes of the reserve team match. I scored a try in both games.

Being out injured so early in my career with Cronulla was the one time in Australia that I went through a period of self-doubt. I was out of action for a number of weeks and, still in the stage of proving myself at the club, I asked Nicola to come out as homesickness took a firm hold.

We had an apartment which overlooked the sea and the view when the electric storms moved in was something else. We would regularly go to the beach and sunbathe and the quality of life there was the best I had experienced. The rugby was hard, as I had expected. Players were better paid than in Britain and the standard of the game was far higher. It was faster, more physical and the professionalism was total. No one was ever late for training and the media coverage was far greater than it had been in Britain. The talk was always straight, whereas at home true feelings were not often vented publicly. There was no holding back in Australia and it made for a healthier atmosphere. One aspect which did strike me as odd was the playing of the Australian national anthem before every game and I virtually knew all the words to Advance Australia Fair by the time I left.

I made eight appearances in my first season, but in 1996 I played in 26 matches. It was a crazy time for the sport with the ARL and Super League sparring in the Australian courts. By the end of 1995, 11 clubs had allied themselves with Super League including Cronulla, Canberra, Auckland and Canterbury. Fixture lists had been drawn up and the players in those clubs who had signed up to ARL were placed elsewhere. ARL had drawn up its fixture list for the 1996 season and it included every club that had previously played in its league. Cronulla did not turn up for their first match against Newcastle, but when ARL's injunction against Super League proved successful, everything returned to normal and Cronulla's ARL players came back into the fold. There were no hard feelings because when it came down to it, both ARL and Super League were paying for loyalty. In fairness to Super League, they did try to keep players informed and every couple of months they would throw a party for us at Darling Harbour where they would reassure us that everything was going according to plan and that their tournament would not be long in kicking off.

Cronulla had two reasonable seasons when I was there, making the play-offs each time. The league was strangely organised: 22 clubs were in it, you played everyone once and three sides twice with the top five going into the play-offs. We finished third in the league in 1995, but we lost to Brisbane after leading 18–0 and we were beaten by Manly the following year, again after appearing to be in control.

Teams never knew when they were beaten in Australia and there was never a time when you could relax. I thrived on that extra competitive edge and I never felt out of my depth.

You had to be careful of the wildlife. I was taking a couple of players back from training one evening in the clapped-out car I drove in Sydney. It had no central locking and as I reached over to the passenger door to let in Brian Laumatia and Tawera Nikau, I noticed a huge spider on the window and panicked. You are quickly warned after arriving in Australia about the deadly spiders which have made their home there, and this specimen looked like something out of a grisly B-movie. The three of us must have made a sight as we jumped about and shouted our heads off. Tawera managed to get the passenger door open and flicked the spider to the ground where I promptly ran over it. It turned out to be harmless, but its appearance was most definitely deceptive. Cockroaches were another menace, forever flying overhead near our apartment, and Sydney was rife with them, which is why the New South Wales side was known as the Cockroaches.

I could not resist the temptation to take a trip to Bateman's Bay and on the way back home I followed a sign saying Kangaroo Valley. It took hours to get to the middle of nowhere with, of course, not a kangaroo to be seen, and as darkness fell you could see bush fires spreading across the mountainside. It was an incredible country, vast and varied. You could be sitting on the beach one minute and driving in the hills through snow the next. Of all the moves I have made, it was the one which was the most fulfilling. The only problem was that we were thousands of miles away from home and while Nicola, Naomi and I had the time of our lives, our families were missing Naomi and there was pressure on us to come back. I had signed a three-year contract with Cronulla and at the end of my first season, I was aware that Warrington wanted to buy me back. I did not want to return there for obvious reasons, but I told Cronulla that if they felt I had not been a good signing for them, I would not hold them to the contract. They said they had no intention of letting me go, but a year later I asked to be released for personal reasons. We were too far away from home. Had it just been Nicola and I, I have no doubt that we would have stayed there for the full three years and perhaps beyond, but Naomi was only four and her grandparents were missing her.

Cronulla were superb to me throughout my time there and they never made any false promises. At the end of 1995, when rugby union turned professional, there was speculation about rugby league players returning to rugby union. As fate would have it, Wales were touring Australia in 1996 and I was told that Terry Cobner, the Welsh Rugby Union's director of rugby, would be seeking me out to have a chat about what I intended to do in the future. One of the players told me that, at a function during the tour, Cobner wangled it so that he was sitting next to me. Unfortunately, he found himself next to the chief executive of Australia's Channel Nine station, another Alan Bateman, but I think he twigged in time.

I turned up at the Wales team hotel when they were staying in Coogee Bay to get some shirts signed. I spoke to a number of the players, but Cobner was nowhere to be seen. I had my father with me because I was taking him back to the airport, and after waving the players on to their bus as they went to training, I tried to get into my old banger, a Mitsubishi Colt that had seen many better days. I could not find the keys and realised that I had locked them in the car. We tried all manner of ways to get in without success and the last thing I wanted was to still be there when the Wales squad got back – and I needed to get to the airport. After a good couple of hours, the hotel janitor pulled off a coat hanger trick and I pulled out on to the road just as the Wales coach was coming up the hill.

In the middle of the 1996 season, I returned to Wales briefly for Wales's international against England in the European championship at Cardiff's Arms Park ground. Australia were playing New Zealand so there was a break in the ARL programme. It meant an exhausting flight, taking off from the north of Queensland, but Nicola reckoned it was worth it because I would be placing myself in the 'shop window' as we looked to move back to Britain. The Australian game had adopted a number of different rules and it was difficult to adjust to the old way. We lost and I wondered if it had all been worth it. I had had to pay for the cost of my flight (later reimbursed by the British rugby league authorities) and there was no match fee. Five weeks after I had returned to Australia, I had a telephone call from my in-laws who said that John Kingston, the Richmond coach, had been asking for my number. He had been looking for an outside-centre and had been given my name by Derek Quinnell.

John called me and I told him that I had another year with Cronulla and would see what they said. Cronulla wanted me to stay but said they would not stand in my way if I wanted to return to Britain. Shortly afterwards, Cobner contacted me and asked what I was doing. I said that I was thinking of signing for Richmond. He asked me not to commit myself to anything and that he would speak to the leading clubs in Wales and tell them that I was available. I heard nothing for a couple of weeks and got in touch with Cobner to tell him that Richmond wanted a decision from me quickly. Cobner said he would get back to me, but I had heard nothing after a week and so I told John that I would be happy to sign. The following day, Llanelli's chief executive Stuart Gallacher faxed me a contract which amounted to virtually the same as Richmond were offering me. I had given a verbal agreement to John Kingston, though, and there was no way I was going back on my word.

I could have been a Llanelli player three times in all. After I had agreed to join Neath in 1989, Llanelli approached me and asked me to go to Stradey Park. I told them they were too late and in 2001, when I was considering my future at Northampton, the Llanelli coach Gareth Jenkins rang me at the beginning of March. He said that Dafydd James, the club's international three-quarter, had told them he would not be renewing his contract at the end of the season – would I be interested in joining on a two-year deal? I would have been but for the fact that the previous day I had told Lyn Jones, the Neath coach, that I would be returning to the Gnoll. I would have fancied playing for Llanelli, a club rich in tradition which plays the game in the right way. Cardiff also came in for me but I could never see myself fitting in there, even though Craig Quinnell had joined them by then. I always saw something aloof and stand-offish about Cardiff, perhaps unfairly, and I never had any ambition to play for them.

My Australian adventure was over. I played my final game against Manly on the Saturday and flew to Britain two days later, arriving on the Wednesday. John asked me if I wanted to have the weekend off, but I wanted to play right away. Our first match was against Newcastle at the Athletic Ground in Richmond; a battle between the two clubs contesting promotion from the second division.

When my in-laws had initially told me that John was trying to get in touch with me, I did not have a clue where Richmond was, a terrible admission considering I had played a few times at London Welsh's Old Deer Park ground, which is less than a mile from Richmond's. It was six years since I had played rugby union and a lot had changed since then. I was sorry to be leaving Sydney and before departing, I made a pact with some of the Cronulla players and friends I had made out there to have a reunion on a Greek island in 2003. It is still on.

SEVEN

REUNION

The two codes of rugby had long been divided by the sporting equivalent of the Berlin Wall. The split came at the end of the nineteenth century after a dispute over broken time: clubs in the north of England felt that players should be reimbursed for wages which they forfeited because of their rugby commitments. There was outrage in the south of England and Wales, and the north went its own way. It is hard to understand now why there was such opposition to broken time which did not amount to the paying of players themselves, but amateurism became a cherished concept, a sacred cow to administrators, even though its spirit had long been flouted.

I was not an amateur when I was at Maesteg. The one pound win bonus broke rugby union's cardinal rule: 'Thou shalt not get any material reward for playing.' The Maesteg club could have been thrown out of the Welsh Rugby Union if the authorities had discovered what was going on and such was the fear of rugby league which had made constant raids on Wales from the 1890s onwards, that anyone who played against a player who had been professionalised was deemed to have contaminated themselves and faced being banned. The history of the WRU reveals a number of instances when clubs were closed down and players suspended for breaches of the amateur regulations, but even though amateurism had glasses raised to it at dinners, there was no way that unions could launch a thorough investigation of their clubs, especially in Wales, because 'brown envelopes' abounded.

Brown envelopes became a euphemism for payment. I could not believe it when I joined Neath because when the players filed into a little office every day for their payments, the cash was indeed stuffed into brown envelopes. It was something everyone laughed and joked about. The money was insignificant, pocket money, and the clubs were easily able to afford it. Looking back now, players were exploited: unions grew rich on the back of their efforts, charging more and more to spectators and receiving more and more from sponsors and broadcasters. Where was the money going though? Back into the grassroots, said the unions, but could the worthy members of committees describe themselves as amateurs in the purest sense with the perks that came with their positions? It was not often that someone volunteered to stand down from the committee, but once the World Cup was introduced in 1987, despite opposition from some of the European unions, the death knell for amateurism had sounded. The game would never be the same again and as the demands on players grew, in terms of time and effort, so it became obvious that issues like broken time needed to be addressed. Concessions were made in order to keep the game nominally amateur, such as trust funds for players (but not coaches), but the administrators were just shoving their fingers in the dyke and it was all too clear that they were going to run out of hands.

When I joined Warrington, rugby league was still the great enemy of rugby union. Wales had suffered more than any other country, with perhaps the exception of Australia, from cheque-book-wielding northerners, and the sanctions against players who went north were stringent because they were meant to act as a deterrent – go north and you became an outcast in your own land, never able to play or coach union again, unwelcome in clubhouses or at grounds and, if you were a former international, you lost your privilege of being able to buy a ticket for a Wales match in Cardiff. The WRU would have probably got the disinfectant out had a rugby league player burst into one of their monthly meetings. While it is easy to understand why the amateurs acted as they did – they could hardly offer money to players to persuade them to stay – the fact that clubs were rewarding players meant that rugby union was living a lie and league officials never missed a chance to make accusations of hypocrisy.

After Wales had won the Triple Crown in 1988, it looked as if we could put the failure of the previous nine years behind us, but one disappointing tour to New Zealand in 1988 led to the coaches being sacked and players leaving for rugby league: Adrian Hadley joined Salford; John Devereux and Paul Moriarty signed for Widnes, soon followed by Jonathan Davies; Rowland Phillips went to Warrington, and David Young was tempted by Leeds after being unable to find a job in Wales. Other internationals joined them: Jonathan Griffiths, Mark Jones, David Bishop and I left, and Terry Holmes, Stuart Evans, Rob Ackerman and Gary Pearce had followed the path north in the middle of the 1980s. Players were driven by the money factor, but not exclusively. There was a concern that the game in Wales was decaying and that unrealistic demands were being placed on players. Nobody was going north because they had a burning ambition to play rugby league; it was simply a job opportunity and many of the league clubs who signed Welsh internationals, in hope more than expectation most of the time, did so because it was an effective way of generating publicity. I must have been an exception because hardly anyone had heard of me in Warrington. When Widnes landed Jonathan Davies, after months of trying, they became the most famous rugby club in Britain for a while having signed one of union's top stars. The fanfare could not have been any greater if Will Carling had changed codes.

There was pressure on Jonathan in a way that there was not on me. All eyes were on him, and it says a lot for his strength of character as well as his rugby ability that he was able to succeed in a sport where he had been tipped to become yet another expensive failure from the valleys. His career in union had ended on a low note after he had led Wales to defeat against Romania in Cardiff in 1988 and he felt that he was being made a scapegoat for the unprecedented reverse with a whispering campaign launched against him. Despite everything he had achieved with Wales, Neath and Llanelli, when he returned to the National Stadium as a radio commentator a few years after joining Widnes, he was refused permission to be interviewed on the pitch as if he would somehow pollute it. Things may have been changing, but the wall did not come tumbling down: it had to be dismantled brick by brick.

The presence of so many Welsh players in rugby league led to the reformation of the Welsh national side in 1991. It had had a chequered history, flourishing when rugby union players were signed up in numbers by league clubs and going into hibernation when there were not enough eligible players to sustain it. There were more than enough of us in 1991 and Clive Griffiths, who was on the coaching staff at Warrington, was appointed coach with Mike Nicholas the manager. Our first match was against Papua New Guinea at the Vetch Field in Swansea and a sell-out crowd greeted our return. I had expected a few thousand at most and the atmosphere was as good as it had been at the Gnoll. We won 66–0 against opponents who a year later were to push Great Britain all the way and, probably to the surprise of the WRU, we were not depicted as mercenaries returning to the ravaged land. It was a firm sign of how attitudes were changing.

The flow of players from Wales to rugby league slowed up in the 1990s – a reflection of the poor form Wales were showing. Ieuan Evans was a target but he could not be tempted away. Several players from Wales used to come up north for trials, which usually involved playing in a reserve team match. Had they been rumbled, as the wing Steve Ford was in the 1980s, they would have been banned from playing rugby union for life. Ford was eventually reinstated and went on to play for Wales, but despite the risks union players continued to try their luck. The reserve matches used to take place on a Friday evening, and one night in 1993 I went along to watch Warrington in action. One player looked familiar to me: he had ginger hair and prominent ears. He scored two tries and landed goals from everywhere. There was a crowd of more than 1,000 there at Wilderspool and some journalists, but the secret of Neil Jenkins never came out. Had it done, the history of Welsh rugby would have been vastly different.

Neil went on to become the leading points scorer in the history of international rugby and the first player to go through the 1,000 barrier. Unlike me, he was a rugby league fanatic who did harbour ambitions about changing codes. Had his appearance in Warrington been reported to the WRU, he would have had no choice but to join a rugby league club, but his exploit stayed undetected and he remained at Pontypridd. Had rugby union not turned professional in 1995, I am sure that he would have become a league player and he had all the attributes to succeed in it. League's loss was very much Wales's gain and Neil was the mainstay of the international side throughout the 1990s and beyond.

Garin Jenkins was another Welsh international who had trials in league and there were other players on the fringes. Steele Lewis, who toured Australia with Wales in 1991, and the hooker Huw Bevan also tried their luck. With so many Welsh players in the north of England, there was little chance of getting homesick and the ones who came up for a trial used to keep us informed about what was going on in Welsh rugby.

Even as the years passed, the regret at not being able to play at the National Stadium still remained. I knew when I made the decision to join Warrington that it was a one-way ticket, but I never gave up hope and returning to the Vetch Field only served to remind us of what we had left behind. It was something that money could not buy – but neither did it pay the mortgage. It became harder and harder to understand why money was such a dirty word in union. I had not questioned it when starting out with Maesteg because it had always been the way and there was no pressure from anyone to change it. Ironically, it was only when England became successful in the 1990s that amateurism was seriously challenged in Europe. Their players, like Will Carling, Brian Moore and Rob Andrew, achieved a profile their predecessors had never threatened to and, as the media took a greater interest in English rugby, so the cream of England questioned why their union should make millions on the back of their efforts and reward them with nothing.

I won 12 caps with Wales in rugby league, together with three for Great Britain. Making the international team in union had taken me five years with a number of knock-backs along the way, but in league it became a case of who was available. We were regarded initially as a team not to be taken too seriously, but it was not long before the European Championship was revived and we won it in 1995, defeating England in one of the highlights of my league career. I have very little recall of the games I have played in. I have always been someone who looks forward rather than backward and one of the things I learned in rugby league was that there was nothing to be gained in dwelling on a defeat. The next game has to be won: you are part of a business, not just a sport, and profitability comes with success. You have to forget about the disappointments and get on with it. Having said that, I do remember the three league internationals I played against England.

The second of these matches was the semi-final of the 1995 rugby league World Cup. Rugby union's version had been played out in South Africa during the summer and Wales had again made up the numbers after changing coaches not long before the tournament started (shades of 1991). While Welsh rugby was in turmoil that autumn, wondering where it was going, the Wales rugby league squad was determined to enjoy the World Cup. Not long after it had started, Wales's coach in the union World Cup, the Australian Alex Evans, had complained that the effort in South Africa had been undermined by players drinking and staying out late at night. Had they been better disciplined, he said, Wales would have made the quarter-finals at least. It was just as well that he was not in charge of the rugby league squad because he would have torn out most of what remained of his hair.

We had a month-long party, drinking virtually every night, except before a game. We were back home and we were determined to enjoy the experience, win or lose. We often stumbled back to our hotel at 3 or 4 a.m. having taken out membership of a casino so that we could carry on drinking after hours. France and Samoa were in our group and we were all aware that in the 1991 rugby union World Cup Samoa (then known as Western Samoa) had sprung the mother of all surprises by defeating Wales at the National Stadium. Even though union had turned professional in August 1995, rugby league was still taboo as far as the WRU was concerned. Other professional sports, like boxing and soccer, were welcome but not rugby league. We played our matches at soccer grounds, the Vetch Field and Cardiff City's Ninian Park, and that probably helped our cause because the grounds were full of vocal supporters while the atmosphere would have been more diluted at the National Stadium.

Our match against Samoa in Swansea was the most physical game of rugby I have ever been involved in. After just five minutes, I was hit in the mouth, accidentally, and for a while I did not know where I was. I have a tape of the match and I can be seen scrabbling around dementedly on the floor, looking for something. A cap on one of my front teeth had been knocked out and eventually I managed to find it. It was one of those nights when you feel every tackle – most of which in this case seemed to be above shoulder height. My Cronulla team-mate, Brian Laumatia, was playing on the wing opposite John Devereux and, after one exchange between the two, Brian went into karate mode, advancing towards John who decided that discretion counted for more than valour and made himself scarce. Brian was like most of the Samoans. They were quiet, God-fearing, gentle men off the field, but on it they seemed to become different personalities and they knew how to make their physical presence count.

Scott Quinnell was magnificent for us that night. He had turned professional in 1994, the greatest loss to Wales since Jonathan Davies went north in 1989, and while it often takes forwards a couple of years to adjust to rugby league, Scott made his presence felt quickly. He took everything the Samoans could throw at him and returned it with interest. It was as satisfying a victory as I could remember and it meant that we had qualified for the semi-finals. England were next up, at Old Trafford. This Manchester United supporter was returning to his field of dreams. I had often watched United while at Warrington, but to play on the ground was something else and I made sure I had a quick tour of the trophy room before the start of the semi-final.

Wales had a strong squad that year with the likes of Iestyn Harris, Keiron Cunningham, Anthony Sullivan, Kelvin Skerrett, Martin Hall and Neil Cowie – league players who qualified for Wales through their parents or grandparents, adding steel and know-how. We were certainly not in it for the money. Our win bonuses for beating France and Samoa were three hundred pounds and nobody made any money out of the month. But we were on the promise of four thousand pounds if we defeated England. League was a game which revolved around bonuses. Every victory at Warrington was worth three hundred pounds, but if we had had a poor run, the club would often double it. It did not make you play any differently and was only something you thought about at the end of a match, but for the local Warrington players it made a big difference because their basic wages were so low.

England proved a match too far for us after the physical demands of the Samoa game, but we proved a point and we were treated in Wales like returning heroes – and it was not to be long before most of us did return, at least to rugby union. We played England again in the 1996 European Championship but lost. A number of the Warrington supporters would support Wales over England because of the strong Welsh presence at Wilderspool, but it gradually became diluted and we have now reached the point where the players who went north have either retired or returned and nobody is tempted away from Wales any more.

My final fling in international rugby league came in Fiji in 1996. The World Nines tournament (league's answer to Sevens) was being staged there. The Welsh squad arrived ahead of me because I had to wait to be released by Cronulla. I flew out with the Australian internationals Andrew Ettingshausen and Paul Green and we landed in the south of the island where we had to get on a coach which took us to our hotel in the north. The journey took a couple of hours, but no sooner had I walked into the hotel than I realised I had left my passport on the bus which was chugging away into the distance. I managed to persuade someone to lend me a car so I could follow the bus which I caught only as it was pulling into the depot. Fortunately, there was only one road on the trail south so there was no chance of the bus losing me, but it was a four-hour diversion in the boiling heat that I could have done without. When I eventually checked in, Clive Griffiths told me to crash out. The previous week, I had played for Cronulla in an exhibition match in Samoa – an attempt to take the game around the islands and persuade locals that it was better than union. It did not stop raining that weekend and it was the same in Fiji where the second day of the Nines had to be called off because of the wettest weather they had had for years.

While we were in Fiji, the High Court in Australia ruled in favour of the Australian Rugby League and against Super League. Rupert Murdoch was about to change the face of British rugby league by introducing Super League: the number of clubs would be cut but those in the tournament would receive vast amounts more money than they had before, and it gave them the means to compete with rugby union clubs who had suddenly become their rivals. But when the time came for me to return to Britain, I was not tempted to go back to Warrington or any other rugby league club. The first port of call would have to have been Warrington because they held my registration (and I still get a letter every year informing me of that fact) – but it was back to union for me and another club I knew nothing about: Richmond.

Cronulla could have made things difficult for me because I still had a year to run on my contract, but they did not demand a transfer fee from Warrington. All they asked for was the return of my $60,000 loyalty bonus (around £30,000). I left that up to Richmond, but I do not think the money was ever paid. Richmond, who were being bankrolled by a millionaire businessman, Ashley Levett, could certainly have afforded it.

The world of union that I returned to was very different from the one I had left. It was professional for a start, a move precipitated by an attempt by the Australian media mogul Kerry Packer to set up a world circus in 1995. He failed to sign up enough players, but enough had made pledges to persuade the unions that they could no longer delay the inevitable and in August 1995, the International Rugby Board announced that the game was going open – 100 years after rugby had split into two codes.

It was ironic that the announcement was made in Paris because France was the one country which had had least regard for amateurism; they'd been banned by the IRB in the past because of payments made to players. When the announcement was made, I did not think it would affect me. I was in my 31st year and I was happy at Cronulla. It was some time after union had abandoned amateurism that it confirmed rugby league players would be free to return and the confusion was not helped by England who immediately announced that they would have a year's moratorium before abandoning it. That created a vacuum which was filled by businessmen such as Ashley Levett (the man who put the 'rich' in Richmond, at least temporarily), Sir John Hall, Nigel Wray, Tom Walkinshaw and Keith Barwell – men who had not been involved in the running of rugby before but who saw the opportunities presented by professionalism. They were not chances which were going to be taken quickly, and having found myself in the middle of a civil war in Australia, I returned to Britain to find another one raging.

The offers that some players were receiving were incredible. The £100,000 I had received from Warrington over five years was far less than many players were getting in one in union. The question in the sport, as far as players were concerned, had used to be, where did the money go? Now it was a case of where was the money coming from? Not that too many bothered posing that one. It was a case of gathering rosebuds while ye may. When I joined Richmond, I thought rugby union in Britain would be bankrupt in five years; instead it was Richmond that went bust.

EIGHT

FOR RICHER BUT NOT POORER

Richmond is a far cry from Maesteg, and not just geographically. It is an area of conspicuous affluence. A detached four-bedroomed house in Caerau, where I was born, would be worth less than a garage in the western fringes of London. Nicola and I bought a house in Esher having left Sydney with our apartment unsold. One of the hazards of being a professional sportsman is that you regularly have to uproot yourself and your family, but travel broadens the mind and I have no doubt that my career would not have been anywhere near as long had I remained with one club.

Richmond was one of the most famous sides in English rugby, founded way back in 1861. It had become synonymous with amateurism and not just because, after Harlequins, it was the closest club to the Twickenham headquarters of the Rugby Football Union. The honours board in the clubhouse was loaded with double-barrelled surnames and there was an old-fashioned air to the Athletic Ground that Richmond shared with London Scottish. When I had been with Maesteg, Welsh club rugby had without any doubt been harder and more physical than the game in England – more professional, dare I say. Bath, who played a number of Welsh sides, developed a layer of steel in the 1980s, but usually when we came to England the people who used to give us the greatest difficulty were the referees. What passed for rucking in Wales was classified as stamping in England and you were guaranteed to lose the penalty count by a considerable margin.

That had all changed by the time I joined Richmond at the end of 1996. England had become the leading national side in Europe and the decision of several businessmen to invest in the club game created a new wealth which attracted players from all over the world. Whereas before professionalism Welsh players went north, now they went east over the Severn Bridge. The Quinnell brothers were at Richmond, along with the international half-backs Adrian Davies and Andy Moore. The prop John Davies joined from Neath as did the Lions' hooker Barry Williams at the end of the 1996–7 season. Adrian and Andy had been among the first players signed by Richmond, joining at the end of the 1995–6 season along with the England and Lions' wing forward Ben Clarke.

Richmond had done very little since the introduction of leagues in England in 1987, muddling along and living in the shadow of Harlequins, a club which was not liked at the Athletic Ground. But while the rivalry between Maesteg and Bridgend, and Neath and Aberavon was very much on the field, the enmity between Richmond and Quins lay more with the administrators than with the players. It was with a wry smile that I read in the summer of 2001 that John Kingston was taking over from Zinzan Brooke as the head coach of Quins. During his time at Richmond, John never wasted a moment to rubbish Harlequins, mainly because of what the club stood for, but when opportunity knocks it does not really matter who is banging at the door.

Richmond had been taken over by Ashley Levett, a businessman based in Monte Carlo. They were in the second division of the league with another big-spending club, Sir John Hall's Newcastle. London became a battleground for bankrollers with Nigel Wray taking over at Saracens and NEC sponsoring Harlequins. Rosslyn Park and Blackheath, two famous sides without backers, went the opposite way and the game became polarised between those who had deep financial resources and those who did not. A problem which no one seemed bothered about at the time was that the money being paid out had not been earned by the clubs. What would happen when the investment ran out and sides had to survive on what they earned? The answer of the investors was to seek to take control of the competitions they played in, but that meant challenging the authority of the Rugby

Football Union as well as the International Rugby Board and barely a day went by without acrimonious exchanges and threats being made in the media.

Levett did not interfere much on the playing side. He watched as many games as he could, but the running of the side, and the club itself as far as I could see, was left to John Kingston. Levett did make one intervention after a match against Gloucester when Scott Quinnell and Barry Williams had been sin-binned. He came into the changing room in a foul mood.

'We would not have lost this game but for two players losing their discipline,' he said. 'From now on, anyone who gets sent to the sin bin gets fined a hundred pounds.' The Quinnell brothers and Barry voiced their objections and Levett, a man used to getting his own way rather than having his authority questioned, bridled and ended up storming out. The threatened sanction never was imposed.

John Kingston was Richmond. He seemed to be in charge of everything, from the smallest playing matters to the biggest decisions on the board. I do not think he trusted anyone to run things as well as he could. There was the legacy of a committee from the amateur days, but Levett had taken the club over completely and there was no interference. John was an excellent coach, but he had an annoying habit of playing mind games with players. When the Wales contingent returned from our Wednesday national training session in Cardiff, he would make us clean balls and pads and make us do other demeaning tasks, even though he had said publicly that he wanted us all to be playing international rugby. He never wasted the opportunity to criticise the then Wales coach Kevin Bowring for rarely coming to Richmond and would rage if one of his players was left out of the Wales side – but at the same time he always let us know who was paying our wages.

We had a pre-season tour to Scotland in 1997 and John called the Quinnells, Barry and myself to one side. He said he had had a complaint that we were trying to take over the club; that we had become unapproachable and were too big for our boots. What surprised me was that the player who had gone to John was the Wales international scrum-half Andy Moore. We went to see him afterwards. He admitted he had approached John and said that other players felt like him, though no one else admitted it. Andy was a smashing bloke and a very good scrum-half. He had been there from the start under Levett, but the arrival of the Argentina international Agustin Pichot had pushed him towards the margins and I think that frustration got the better of him.

Richmond was a side thrown together. The club had had little ambition before Levett, but suddenly they had their eyes on the top division and Europe. They became big players overnight thanks to a rich man's largesse and it meant they had to recruit virtually a full side. Ben Clarke had been arguably the club's biggest signing. The England international had toured New Zealand in 1993 with the Lions and he was the obvious choice to be made captain. He was a strong character, but he had the capacity to rub players up the wrong way. The best way I can describe him is that he liked the players he liked and the rest he wanted nothing to do with. Pichot found himself blanked by Ben to the point where the captain and back-rower would not speak to his scrum-half and would be aggressive towards him in training. Pichot once asked me what he could do about it; he felt scared and intimidated and all I could tell him was to get on with it. Ben was a friend of Andy Moore's, the player Pichot had ousted from the side, and there was no way he was going to do the Argentine any favours.

Players would often take a pop at Ben in training, much to the amusement of John Kingston – who, like Ron Waldron during my time at Neath, encouraged fierce rivalry between players. Barry Williams had a real go at Ben one morning, landing a couple of punches on him and pinning him on the floor while John laughed his head off. Scott Quinnell got on well with Clarke even though they were both number 8s by preference. They came to an arrangement often whereby Scott would lead the attack from number 8 and Ben would go there in defensive positions, a compromise which worked well. Clarke was a big player for Richmond who remained loyal to the club until its sad and premature end as a professional entity.

We won the second division title to gain the promotion that Levett so craved. Money was thrown at us that season: £200 for every win even though most of the sides we were up against were unable to start to compete with us financially. We each received

£10,000 for finishing on the top of the second division and it seemed to be worth getting relegated the following season to have another crack at that bonus. There were no win bonuses when we were in the top division which made Richmond the opposite of Warrington. There were constant rumours about Levett's commitment to the club – that he wanted other investors to come on board but could not find any takers and that he was angry at the local council for refusing to give him planning permission to develop the ground. We played out the final season at the Madejski Stadium in Reading, a brave move which had just about succeeded by the time Levett pulled the plug.

We made the semi-final of the English Cup in 1996–7 and faced Sale for the right to a day out at Twickenham. It was a match we should have won. Our hooker, Brian Moore, the former England international who was playing for us on an amateur basis, was sent off for stamping – a decision which beggared belief. After looking at the video, it seemed clear that he was rucking for a ball which was very much on our side. Even with a man short, we still looked like holding out until the wing David Rees scored a try in the final minute of the match to deny us the perfect end to what had been, by the standards of Richmond since the introduction of leagues, a remarkable campaign. Our only rivals were Newcastle. My first match for the club had been the home fixture against them. We were leading 20–13 with only a couple of minutes to go and were under our own posts. Andy Moore passed the ball to me and I went to kick it to touch. Kicking is not the strongest feature of my game and the ball failed to make it by a couple of yards. It had distance though and when the wing Tony Underwood caught it 45 yards out from our line, I did not think we were in any danger. A few seconds later Gary Armstrong scored the try which tied the match and I was left looking shame-faced.

When I returned to Richmond, I did not hold out much hope of being recalled by Wales. I was 31 and Wales were not struggling for centres with Leigh Davies and Gareth Thomas making an impact – and with Scott Gibbs, who was six years younger than me, also returning from rugby league. Stuart Barnes, the former England outside-half who was a columnist for the *Daily Telegraph* and a summariser for Sky Sports who had the rights to televise club rugby in England, advanced my cause. I would like to think it had something to do with the way I was playing, but he had been in a bar in Richmond one evening when some big guy was having a go at him and I waded in. I am not sure that the heavy was too worried by my intervention, but when he saw Scott and Craig Quinnell looming behind me, he remembered that he had somewhere else to go and bade his farewells.

My first return for a club match in Wales came in 1997 when Richmond came to Bridgend, the ground where 19 years before I had watched a club for the first time. Bridgend were taking on the All Blacks that time and J.P.R. Williams got a boot in the head for his pains. The Brewery Field was packed back then, but there was no crush at the turnstiles for Richmond's European Conference match there. It struck me then how much had changed in the Welsh game in the seven years I had been away: while the national team still had passionate and avid supporters, clubs were struggling to make ends meet and there were barely a couple of thousand spectators in Bridgend for Richmond's victory, a far cry from the day when fans climbed up the floodlight pylons at the Gnoll.

We did not make a major impact in our two years in the top division, holding our own without threatening to win the title. We made the English Cup semi-final in 1999 after beating Leicester at the Madejski Stadium, but we knew by then that the club was unlikely to survive to fight another season. Ashley Levett announced that he was withdrawing his backing and Richmond, along with London Scottish, was cannibalised by the other first division clubs in an episode which reflected badly on the game in England. The feelings of supporters and the livelihoods of players were trampled underfoot in an unseemly dash for cash.

It was hardest on John Kingston who had fought so hard to make Levett's dream work. He was not that popular among the players because of his penchant for playing mind games and because his man-management left something to be desired. As a coach, he was out of the top drawer. He was a meticulous planner and made sure that we were fully prepared going into games, but because he had had to sign so many players at the same time and because Richmond was very much a multi-national side, egos were going to be trodden on and tensions often surfaced. Levett had been clever in choosing the players he had assembled because most of us did not command a transfer fee. Their biggest outlay was the £250,000 they paid Wigan for Scott Quinnell and it meant they could invest more in wages.

In December 1998, a number of players, led by Pichot, Matt Pini and Jason Wright, called a meeting. They wanted to propose a vote of no-confidence in John and his two coaches, Mark Tainton and Rob Lozowski. They felt that the three were not up to it and that the club was drifting as far as the playing side of things went. I tried to persuade them not to go ahead with it, saying that it would achieve nothing and would only cause ill-feeling which would ultimately undermine us. They were having none of that though and insisted that they be allowed to air their feelings and to take steps to get rid of John. The meeting was called and John was invited. When he came into the room, he did not have a clue what was going on and his face dropped when he realised what was on the agenda.

The discontented players had their say. Craig Quinnell got up and said that while he may have agreed with some of the points that had been put, he pointed out that it was not an old-fashioned committee meeting where votes of no-confidence were common. John was a professional rugby coach and if there were grievances there were proper channels to go through. John got up and walked out, saying that he was not going anywhere. As an exercise it was pointless because nothing happened but it did serve to show how rugby union had changed and illustrated the problems that were associated with a large, eclectic squad, especially when there was not success on the field. Pichot was the prime mover even though he owed his position in the side to John. He was an enigma as a player and as a person he was very talented but temperamental. He liked to get his own way.

In the end, John fell with the players and the club. The end was quick in coming: one minute we were preparing for our English Cup quarter-final against Leicester in Reading, and the next the club had been put into administration because of Levett's decision to withdraw his backing. The move to the Madejski Stadium had been a success. We kept the majority of the supporters who had watched us at Richmond and attracted a number of new ones. There was no doubt that there were companies in the Reading area willing to invest in the club, but EFDR decided that it wanted the number of sides in the top flight cut and with London Scottish also in financial trouble, it could get rid of two at a stroke.

It was a cynical and disgraceful way to treat people. The players immediately had their wages cut by 20 per cent and there was no guarantee we would even get that much. The club president, Tony Dorman, a genuine man of the old school, promised me that he would pay me himself if he had to, but the moment that EFDR made it plain that there was to be no future for Richmond (despite the fact that at least two consortia were raising the money to buy the club), players started looking elsewhere and the cup semi-final held precious little in the way of significance: Newcastle beat us at a canter with Va'aiga Tuigamala offering a physical threat that we were not up to containing. It was not so bad for the players: we could always find new employers. The ones I felt for were the backroom staff at Richmond, people with an emotional investment in the club. They had been stabbed in the back by people without a real feel for the game, in the name of business. The players blamed EFDR rather than Levett, but three years hardly amounted to a significant investment in terms of time, and the question had to be asked what Levett had come into the game for.

All the players found new homes in the end and ironically many of us ended up at clubs whose owners had pulled the plug on Richmond – beggars can't be choosers. John had put on a brave face, saying that he was going to carry on regardless, but he knew that the game was up. The administrators said publicly that a rescue package would be put together, but there was nothing they could do about EFDR. It was a desperate time for the supporters as well. They had been very loyal and the players had made a point after matches of going into their bar to socialise rather than mixing with sponsors. The last couple of months were a nightmare: a famous club being stripped of its future and it was upsetting when we had to say our goodbyes to the office staff and everyone who worked at the club. There have been reunions, but the sense of bitterness will take a long time to subside.

I wondered if anyone would be interested in me. I was 34 and, though I was still in the Wales squad, I hardly represented an investment in the future. I soon found myself in demand. Newport approached me, along with Bristol who were then coached by Bob Dwyer who had guided Australia to World Cup success in 1991. I met Dwyer and discussed terms with him and Newport also made me an attractive offer. The problem with both clubs was that they were in the stages of rebuilding and since I was at the stage of my career when I was a lot closer to the end than the beginning, I wanted to join a side which would be able to challenge for trophies. Newport at that stage were at the foot of Wales's premier division, but within the coming months they were to sign a number of internationals, starting with Peter Rogers and ending with the former South Africa skipper Gary Teichmann. They admitted that it was going to take them at least a couple of years to rebuild and I did not feel that I had that long.

It was a different story when Northampton approached me. I met their coach Ian McGeechan, who I had got to know on the 1997 Lions tour to South Africa, and I said yes to him straight away even though the financial package was no better than those offered by Bristol and Newport. The money was not my prime motivation though. McGeechan had assembled a strong squad at Northampton, they were in the Heineken Cup unlike Bristol and Newport, and they were a club ready to challenge for silverware immediately. I told Dwyer that I would not be joining Bristol and he exploded.

'What do you mean? You agreed to join us,' he said. It was not true: had I given Bristol a verbal assurance I would have gone there. All I had said was that the terms they offered me were acceptable. I had not committed myself. It was flattering to have clubs fighting over me, but I would still have liked to have had the chance to see my career out at Richmond. Nicola and I were happy living in Esher and the quality of life was excellent. EFDR's actions meant we had to scour the newspaper property columns again. I signed a two-year contract with Northampton, looking forward to working with McGeechan again, though by the time I arrived at Franklin's Gardens he had gone to take up the job of Scotland national coach. He was one of my reasons for joining Northampton: I would have gone there anyway, but Geech is probably the best coach I have played under and even at 34 there was still a lot for me to learn.

NINE

TEACHER'S PET

Rugby union had changed considerably on the field in the six years I had been away. It was faster and more physical and new law changes had opened the game up and made it more enjoyable for players. With the ball-in-play time increasing, there was more involvement than there had been and whereas emphasis in past days had often been on the negative, killing the ball and slowing things down, now tactics revolved around keeping possession and taking play through several phases, probing for openings. It was partly a consequence of professionalism, with players having as much time as they wanted to concentrate on fitness, but it was also because those running clubs realised the importance of attracting crowds. As admission charges went up, so sides realised they had to justify taking the supporters' money and that meant, amongst other things, offering a spectacle.

The return of players from rugby league generated considerable publicity. Our mass departure had been held up as one of the excuses for Wales's decline. In the six Five Nations Championships that I had missed, Wales had won seven matches out of twenty-four – three in one season – and with the likes of Scott Gibbs, Scott Quinnell, Jonathan Davies and David Young coming back into the fold, there was a renewed sense of optimism. In a sense it was misplaced, because Wales's decline preceded our departures, but the exodus had not helped. Kevin Bowring had taken over as the Wales coach after the 1995 World Cup, and his first championship in charge had seen

Wales improve considerably in terms of performance on the previous year but not so much in terms of results. It was felt that the professionalism of the rugby league players would harden up Wales and help turn narrow defeats into victories.

Professionalism in union seemed to revolve around pay rather than attitude. I was surprised at the high rates of pay: six-figure contracts were offered with abandon, virtually double the wages of established rugby league players. It reflected the involvement of benefactors in union, but it meant that salary levels, which were not weighted towards bonuses, were unrealistic. Wales were one of the first countries to put their squad players under contract, but it led to complications because players also had a contract with their clubs. As the various factions in the sport started falling out, the players became caught in the middle of the conflict, none more so than the Welsh contingent at Richmond.

The Welsh Rugby Union adopted a policy of rewarding national squad players according to where they played their rugby. Those based in Wales received considerably more than those of us who earned our livings in England. It was easy to understand the reason behind the move. The WRU was anxious to keep its leading players in Wales and, whereas it was unable to act when it came to preventing anyone taking up an offer from rugby league other than to make them an outcast, it had the resources to keep them from the clutches from union clubs in England and France and made full use of them.

It was a divisive policy nevertheless and it meant that some players got more than others for doing the same job. Scott Quinnell, and his agent Mike Burton, were particularly unhappy, and not without reason. Richmond, not the WRU, had paid the £250,000 to get Scott back from Wigan and ensure that he was available to play for Wales again. It did not just extend to what contracts were worth. When the WRU signed a kit deal with Reebok, players were told they had to wear that company's boots in international matches. Scott had a deal with Puma, but he was told that unless he wore Reebok boots, he would not be picked. Craig also had a contract with Puma and he attempted to get round the problem by blacking out the maker's name on his boots and painting on Reebok stripes. Puma found out and told him to cut it out.

As the Richmond players' national contracts were worth £10,000 a year, compared to the £40,000 that some players in Wales were commanding, Scott decided to go on international strike in the autumn of 1997 and he refused to make himself available for Wales. I am not sure whether the idea was Scott's or Burton's, but it was an understandable reaction. In rugby league, players at international level received the same and you were essentially paid for winning. Yet we had a situation with Wales where even the most unsuccessful season on record would still prove lucrative for some players who were based there. Even the bonuses and appearance money for Wales were different according to where you played. It was a form of apartheid and it fostered resentment. It never made me think that I should be playing in Wales, though, because I was happy where I was.

I signed a three-year deal with Wales that was worth £20,000 annually. Barry Williams, who had joined Richmond in the summer of 1997, received £15,000. Scott eventually signed before the start of the 1998 championship season, but he never told me what he had been offered. He had ended his strike at the start of the 1997 Five Nations and eventually won the right to wear the boots he wanted. I had worn Puma boots, though unlike Scott I did not have a contract with the company. They did pay me and provide kit, but after the Lions tour of South Africa in 1997, I switched to Mizuno. Reebok had by then backed down from their stance of insisting that all the national squad players wore their boots, something which had been deeply unpopular with many squad members who were based in Wales.

As I was closer to 32 than 30 when I returned to play rugby union, I did not give much thought to playing for Wales again. I knew that they might be interested in me because Terry Cobner had been determined to get me back from Cronulla, but the next World Cup was not until 1999 and I presumed I would be deemed too old to appear there. Scott Gibbs was the first of the rugby league players to get back into the international fold: less than two months after returning to Swansea from St Helens, he was playing for Wales against Italy in Rome. In another two months he would be leading his country.

In the autumn of 1996, I was invited to play for the Barbarians against Australia at Twickenham, along with the Quinnell brothers and Andy Moore from Richmond. I had been invited to train with Wales, but it was only after the match against the Wallabies that I was chosen for the national squad. Wales played Australia at the beginning of December and ended up losing a closely contested match. Two weeks later, they were playing South Africa at the National Stadium and I was chosen for the team because of an injury to Gareth Thomas. I found myself partnering Scott Gibbs for only the third time in a union match, more than seven years after our last appearance together. The Springboks were a slightly tougher test than Abertillery had been and they won 37–20 thanks to a hat-trick of tries by their scrum-half Joost van der Westhuizen.

I got on very well with Kevin Bowring. He had some excellent ideas and Wales played some excellent rugby under him, but he had two weaknesses which ultimately undermined him. He had never coached a senior club in Wales and was not prepared for many of the pressures that come with the job of the national coach, especially when the media started gunning for him. He was also a former teacher who irritated a number of players by tending to talk down to them. He gave orders and commands where others would have coaxed and cajoled. He always spoke to me on a proper level, perhaps because he trusted me to do things right whereas he could not be so sure with others. There were players he would always look to rein in, like Arwel Thomas, Craig Quinnell, Gareth Thomas and Chris Wyatt. These were individuals who liked to be given a long lead but that lead grew shorter and shorter as the pressure on Bowring mounted.

Every time Bowring saw Craig, he would ask how heavy he was. Craig had made his international debut against Fiji in November 1995 as a back-row forward. Blessed with good hands and vision, Craig was an outstanding blind-side flanker, but his size soon saw him converted to the second row. He came to develop a complex about his weight and there were many snide remarks about his fitness or alleged lack of it. Craig is a happy-go-lucky character, but the insults got to him. Bowring did not really know how to handle him and ended up getting far less out of a talented player than he should have. When Graham Henry took over as the Wales coach in August

1998, Craig immediately came to the fore. Like Bowring, Henry had been a teacher, but the difference between the two was that Henry did not talk down to players and treated them as equals.

Bowring did make a point of telling players why they had been left out of the side, something that many of his predecessors had not been good at, and I have no doubt that he deserved to be given the chance to coach Wales. His main problem, something that Henry was not to suffer, was that he was not given much support by the WRU. The game was going through enormous changes with the Union struggling to keep up with events, but Bowring was paid far less money than the players he was working with. When Henry came over from New Zealand, he was given a salary which was five times greater than his predecessor's. Bowring needed someone on the WRU's general committee to argue his case, as Henry was to have in David Pickering who took over as the team manager of Wales in August 1998. Bowring's ideas on how the game should be structured were sound, but his views carried no weight with the Union and he was always blowing into the wind.

Although the players called me 'Golden Bollocks' because I got on so well with Bowring, Bowring's relationship with John Kingston deteriorated so badly that he stopped coming to Richmond to watch the Welsh contingent in action. When I was invited to play for Wales in the World Cup Sevens in Hong Kong in 1997, Kingston did not want me to go, and when Wales played Romania at Wrexham in August 1997, he tried to persuade Barry Williams and me to pull out, saying that it was not a hard game and that Richmond's match against Saracens the following day was far more important. Having just won promotion, Kingston wanted us to make an impact in the top division and he was right in the sense that Romania were never going to run Wales close.

He was wrong, though, to effectively ask players to choose between club and country. No matter how badly we felt the WRU had treated us, we were not going to turn our backs on Wales, despite Scott Quinnell's protest – but Kingston was not to be denied. He said that Barry and I had to play against Saracens on the Sunday. That meant not only playing two matches in two days, but it also meant driving from North Wales to London on the Saturday night. We duly overwhelmed Romania 70–21 and I scored two tries, my first for Wales at home. Barry would have had two as well, but he celebrated scoring one of them before he had touched it down and it was pushed out of his hands. The drive back was a long one, and when we woke up on the Sunday morning we found out it had been a wasted journey. Princess Diana had died in a car accident in Paris and all sporting events that day were called off as a mark of respect.

Kingston constantly complained that Bowring did not watch Richmond, but his job meant he often had to put club before country and I found myself caught up in another row at the end of that season. Wales were touring South Africa, a year after the Lions' successful mission there, and I was chosen in the squad. I had injured my nose the previous Christmas and it required surgery. Richmond wanted me to have it at the end of the season so that I would be fit for the start of the next one but Wales wanted me to hold on until I returned from South Africa. That would have meant missing the opening month of the new campaign and Kingston was not prepared to accept that. I felt angry that I had been placed in such a position because it meant I had to choose between club and country.

I could not see the point of the tour anyway. The players were worn out after two hard years and Scott Gibbs and Neil Jenkins, who had been central to the Lions' success, were not going because of injuries. I felt the WRU should have downgraded it to a development tour, and so did many other players. We were going to be on a hiding to nothing, all the more so when Bowring resigned as national coach after the 1998 Five Nations campaign. It meant that caretaker coaches were going to be in charge in South Africa and nothing was going to be gained or learned from the trip. In the end, Wales relented and I had my operation. The Wales flanker Colin Charvis, one of those who did make the trip, criticised those who had pulled out, but the point was that the administrators were asking far too much of the players. As the game became more and more physically intense, so rest periods became more crucial but those running the game seemed to be intent on playing internationals every month in the dash for cash.

If Wales had told me to go to South Africa, I would have. As a rugby player, there is nothing more rewarding, in a playing sense, than representing your country. At my age, I had been pleased to be chosen for the squad. I treated every match as if it was going to be my last, grateful to have the opportunity. I had played in the 1997 and 1998 Five Nations campaigns and with the World Cup, which was being hosted by Wales, little more than a year away, I did not want to jeopardise my chances of selection. Kingston had put me in an awkward position, and while I could see his argument – Richmond were my employers and they were paying for the operation – he should have been more sensitive to my predicament.

The two championship seasons had been eventful. My first match back was against Scotland at Murrayfield, a ground where Wales had not won since 1985. We breezed home 34–19 and much was made of Scott Quinnell's try because Scott Gibbs and I had been involved in its build-up. It was taken as evidence of what Wales were now capable of with their rugby league players back in harness, and when we scored a try in the first minute at home to Ireland in the following match (a game I missed because of a knee cartilage problem) there were thoughts of the Triple Crown. But there is something about playing Ireland in Cardiff, a ground where they had not lost for 14 years. They fought back and Neil Jenkins, playing out of position at full-back, where he was to shine for the Lions that summer, was unlucky under a high ball when he tried to touch it down against a post. Ireland scored and we lost 26–25.

Our next match was also close. We had not beaten France in Paris since 1975 and this was to be our last chance here because they were moving to a new ground in the north of the city. Neil again had some unfortunate bounces and we lost 27–22. Had Jonathan Humphreys not knocked on with the line at his mercy, we would probably have won. Of all the championship matches I have played in, it was probably the best in terms of performance. We took the game to France and scored three tries, but we just lacked that killer instinct, even though Arwel Thomas, probably the smallest player on the field, decked Philippe Carbonneau with a corking punch. We collapsed in the final game against England, ravaged by injuries, but Jonathan Davies at least had the honour of becoming the player to score the final points at the National Stadium before it was demolished to make way for a new stadium in time for the 1999 World Cup.

England were our first opponents in 1998, ten years on from our last victory at Twickenham. We had been bullish in our build-up to the match and we were all over them in the first 20 minutes. I scored two tries and our 12–6 lead did not do us justice. The game then turned when England were awarded a penalty which should have gone to us. They kicked for touch, drove the lineout and then scored from the resulting scrum. Our defence collapsed and Neil Jenkins was exposed at full-back. Scott Gibbs and I virtually lost contact with each other in the centre. He was trying to protect the outside-half Arwel Thomas, who had been carrying an injury, and the result was a huge gap which England ran through. Bowring should have taken Arwel off and moved Neil from outside-half, but everyone was bewildered by the speed with which the match turned around and our 60–26 defeat was the worst of any side in the history of the championship.

The dressing-room was a depressing place to be afterwards. We had thought we had a good chance of beating England, but we were blown apart. I think that it was a case of it being 'one of those days' and that we could have turned around and beaten them the following week. But Kevin Bowring took the defeat hard and as we prepared for our next match against Ireland at Wembley, he virtually banned all contact with the media. The pressure was on and we knew it. Bowring knew that his position was under threat, and he transmitted the tension he felt to the players. Despite that, we beat Scotland in a poor match and then defeated Ireland at Lansdowne Road. England had not been forgotten, but we had salvaged something from the season. We changed our tactics: Neil replaced Arwel at outside-half and we played more of a percentage game and tightened up in defence.

France, at Wembley, were our final opponents. When the National Stadium was knocked down, there was nowhere in the principality for Wales to play and Wembley was seen as the only option. Our first game there had been against New Zealand at the end of 1997 and I was surprised at the atmosphere generated at the ground. We were well beaten, but we matched them in the second half and the crowd kept us going. France were coming to north London in search of their second successive Grand Slam and we were hit by injuries: the wrong opposition at the wrong time.

I was chosen to play and I was about to set off from my home on the Monday for training when we had a call from Naomi's school. When I am going to be away with Wales for a week or more, we allow Naomi to stay up later than normal on the last night. When the school said that Naomi had bumped her head, I put it down to the fact that she was tired and went to pick her up. Her teacher also said that Naomi's writing had become vertical rather than horizontal but when we got Naomi home, it became clear that there was something seriously wrong. I gave her a book with large print to read and she could not make out anything, complaining that it was all blurry.

We took her to the surgery where the doctors put the vision problem down to an epileptic episode and said it would pass. By now, Naomi could not see but it was her temperature they checked rather than her eyes. I rang the casualty department at Kingston Hospital. We had to wait for five very long hours before seeing anyone. Naomi picked up a toy gorilla but could not make out what it was. The gorilla was holding a CD and when I asked her what it was, she replied that it felt like a coconut. The hospital had an eye emergency unit, and when we eventually saw a specialist, he told us that Naomi's optic nerves had swollen up to five times their normal size. He said that it was unusual to have the nerves in both eyes affected at the same time. He said that the problem was either a brain tumour or pressure in the spinal column producing pressure in the brain. Naomi needed tests and an MRI scan.

There was no way that I could play against France and I told the Wales management. It was a frightening experience, made worse by the fact that we did not know what was wrong with Naomi. It was impossible to sleep and one day dragged into the next, eyes kept open by shots of coffee. The MRI scan meant Naomi had to be pushed into a machine, unable to see what was going on. She was given some valium to calm her down, but it had the opposite effect and made her hyper. It was hours before we got her in, but thankfully the result proved negative.

On the fourth day we went to London for the test on Naomi's spine. That involved pushing a large needle into the base of her spine and withdrawing fluid. Nicola did not like the idea of it and burst from the room in tears. The doctor said we should curl Naomi up into a ball when the needle went in, which I did. Before the doctor had started, I told Naomi to shout and she did, asking me why I was letting the doctor hurt her. Nicola, who was sitting outside, thought that Naomi was in agony and got into a terrible state. The test again proved negative and the diagnosis then was that it had to be optic-neuritis. Naomi had to be fed an intravenous drip of steroids for two days and that was probably the hardest point – they made her depressed. Nicola and I stayed by her bed for the whole time and gradually her sight started getting better.

It was six months before Naomi enjoyed normal vision again, but we were assured that there would be no permanent damage. I was overwhelmed with letters and cards which poured in from all over the world. A group of Warrington supporters clubbed together and bought a giant cuddly teddy bear and one of them, known to everyone as 'Cullo', travelled to London on the day of his daughter's 18th birthday to present it to Naomi – a moving gesture we have never forgotten. One Welsh rugby follower had contacted me via Mike Burton. He ran an eye clinic in New York City and offered to treat Naomi there. I thanked him for his very generous offer, but wrote that the treatment was working. The improvement over the first two weeks had been marked, but it slowed after that. No one knew how or why the problem had arisen; the theory was that it was an air-borne virus which Naomi probably caught at school and that there was no reason why it should occur again. Naomi, who was six at the time, had taken it in her stride and was far calmer than her parents.

The France match proved the end for Kevin Bowring. Thomas Castaignède enjoyed the type of game you dream about and Wales lost 51–0. It was the end for Bowring. He said that he wanted to carry on in charge and made a list of recommendations to the WRU about the structure of the game in Wales. The Union said there was nothing they could do and they parted company with their coach, something that had happened far too often in the previous ten years. The WRU seemed to see the solution in terms of one man, when it was clear that the problems ran far deeper than that and Bowring was always fighting a losing battle.

Bowring tried to get more for the players but he never had the authority to go with his position. His overall record was not that bad, but he had to take everything on his shoulders and it wore him down. He was a decent man with a sharp rugby brain, someone who undoubtedly had a role to play with the national team, but he could not battle against the system and by the end he was unable to absorb the pressure. He passed it on to the players and would get sharp with them. We were warned about the media and a black cloud seemed to be permanently hanging over the squad. The prospect of touring South Africa was looming and it was the right time for Bowring to go, not because of any deficiencies he had as a coach but because he had been put in a position where he was clearly seen not to be in charge of his own destiny.

I always got on well with him and I owe him a debt of gratitude because he resurrected my international career at a time when other coaches may have considered me too old. At the end of the 1998 season, I was on a shortlist of five for the European player of the year along with Castaignède, Christian Califano, Philippe Carbonneau and Neil Back. The winner was announced at a dinner in London and after his performance against Wales, Castaignède was the runaway victor. I had been amazed to be nominated and even though I did not win, it was one of the proudest moments of my career. Craig Quinnell accompanied me to the dinner. I was presented with a trophy and Craig made me carry a life-size photo of myself around London. I had intended to get away from the function early but ended up the worse for wear. Craig looked after the trophy for me, but the photo ended up in a pub – it is still there!

TEN

ROAR DEAL

One of my regrets when I signed for Warrington was that I would never be able to play for the British and Irish Lions, the pinnacle in the career of a player from the four home unions. When the Lions toured New Zealand in 1993, with Scott Gibbs one of their successes, I felt envious. All that eluded Jonathan Davies in his successful career in both codes was a tour with the Lions. He signed for Widnes five months before the 1989 trip to Australia on which, I have no doubt, he would have been one of the leading players. The Lions would have toured in 1986 but for the sporting boycott of South Africa and for Jonathan it was not to be.

It appeared that way for me after I had turned professional. Whereas Jonathan would have been a certainty in 1989, there was no way I could have said that I would have been chosen in the squad for New Zealand – but it would have been something to aim for. When I joined Richmond in 1996, it was a Lions' year with South Africa the destination in the summer of 1997. I could not look that far ahead because I had to prove myself in union again, get back into the Wales team and show that I was capable of playing international rugby. I thought that I had too much to do and that South Africa was coming a year early for me, even allowing for the fact I was 32. That may have been the case but for the decision of the Barbarians to choose me against Australia and then also the mouth injury which forced Gareth Thomas to withdraw from the Wales team to face South Africa soon afterwards.

Ian McGeechan had been appointed the coach of the Lions for the third successive year and he welcomed the return of players from rugby league. A number of the backs who went to South Africa had been professionals for more than two years and Geech saw that as a strength. John Bentley, Alan Tait, Scott Gibbs, David Young, Scott Quinnell and I were all chosen, but Jim Telfer, who was in charge of the forwards, seemed less enraptured by the league effect and David was to become shamefully treated like an outcast, the one negative aspect of what was a highly successful and memorable tour.

Selection effectively hinged on the 1997 championship and Wales could not have made a better start, with a handsome victory in Scotland. The following week, I was playing for Richmond against Bedford when I was tackled by the former Wales full-back Mike Rayer. My knee became trapped and I cried out in pain. I was helped off the field and thought that my hopes of going to South Africa had ended. I had an operation the following Tuesday to remove a piece of cartilage and I was running within five days. I had no chance of playing against Ireland, but the France international in Paris two weeks later was a distant dream. It was a race against time, but Kevin Bowring said he would give me as long as he could to prove my fitness and he was true to his word. I played against France and England and was chosen in the 35 for South Africa.

I thought at the time that I had a good chance of being selected, but you should never expect anything. The selection process has always been said to have an element of horse-trading between the countries and it is not always a question of form. In 2001, I did not expect to go to Australia, even though I had been chosen in the provisional squad of 67. It was not just my age (I had just celebrated my 36th birthday, though 'celebrated' is probably the wrong word to use as I was looking to negotiate a new contract at the time) but I could not see myself getting a place in the centre or on the wing. Versatility was an advantage, but I had not started a championship match for Wales that year, making just two appearances from the bench, and there were several others ahead of me. I ended up being chosen for the Wales tour to Japan instead, and while Scott Gibbs reacted to the disappointment of being left out of the Lions' squad by saying that he did not want to go to Japan, my reaction was totally different.

I thought Scott's stance was wrong, though it was understandable because he had expected to go to Australia, whereas I had thought that making the 67 was an achievement in itself. When it comes to playing for your country, there should be no picking and choosing. In 1997, Phil de Glanville, the England captain, had missed out; being dropped is an occupational hazard in sport and it is important that you react positively to it. I could understand Scott's feeling of devastation – he had been the man of the series in South Africa in 1997 and he was a player of proven world class, but by saying that he did not want to go to Japan he was implying that a Wales tour was not important and that should never be the case. Japan may have been more appealing to me because I had set my sights lower than Scott, but he is someone young players look up to and he had a role to play on the Wales tour. Scott is very much his own man, and even though we both appeared in the centre for Neath back in 1990, it was only in the 2000–01 season that I started to get to know him. He is a private man and very deep: a problem with international weeks is that while the players are herded together in hotels and can hardly avoid each other's company, you end up talking trivia for the most part and rarely get to the point where you can appreciate what makes someone tick. You try to laugh away nervous energy and I am sure we will all look back in our retirement years and remember little of what we did between matches.

I knew that my rival for the 1997 Test spot at outside-centre would be Bath's Jeremy Guscott, a survivor of the 1989 and 1993 tours. I rated him as the best attacking centre in the world, a player of sublime talents who had had the misfortune to play in an England team which, for the most part, did not seek to exploit his talents to the full. England were then a conservative side, playing the percentages. They were powerful and efficient, a total contrast to the weak-willed teams that came to Wales in the 1970s and 1980s – but Guscott had so much to offer that it seemed a waste when he would come from the field with barely a stain on his jersey. I had first encountered him in the 1980s when Maesteg played at Bath. It was Nicola's birthday and I proposed to her. My memory tells me that Guscott played at outside-half that day. Wherever he was, he made an impression on me and he developed into an international player of the highest class.

The choice for the Lions' selectors was whether they wanted an attacking outside centre (which meant Guscott) or whether they intended to concentrate more on defence, which would have given me the advantage. In the event, they opted for offence – something I could not understand at the time. Despite his lack of opportunities in attack, though, he did drop the goal which clinched the series in Durban. You can never keep a good man down.

While Guscott was a prince among players, he could be difficult to get on with off the field. He had a reputation for trying to disorient team-mates, throwing them curve balls to see how they would react, almost like an amateur psychologist. I roomed with him early in the tour and we got on amicably, but Neil Jenkins had a problem a few weeks later when they were sharing a room. Jerry was sitting on his bed when Neil came into the room. He looked at Neil and said: 'If you are looking for someone to speak to, don't bother talking to me. Have a chat with one of your Welsh mates instead.' Neil is as nice a guy as you could hope to meet and he was taken aback. It took him a long time to tell anyone about the incident which was not only inexplicable but which also flew in the face of the main tour objective which was to mould four nationalities into one. I only ever saw the good side of Jerry, but he did sometimes cast a shadow as Neil found out. There were other Welshmen on the tour who may have reacted differently to Neil then, who merely walked out of the room and closed the door quietly behind him.

The first meeting of the Lions had been in Birmingham where all the 65 players chosen in the provisional squad gathered for a fitting. The Quinnell brothers and I drove up from London. It was the week before the England international and we were going from the fitting to a Wales training session. I did the driving, and just before the tunnel on the Monmouth road I was stopped by the police for speeding. I was doing 80 mph in a 70 mph area and it cost me forty pounds and three points on my licence. The policeman recognised the three of us and asked the Quinnells for their autographs. They looked at the officer in disbelief and replied in the negative.

I cannot remember how I learned that I was in the squad. My recollection is that I read it on teletext, but other players say they had a letter. In 2001, I learned I was not going through the radio. When you are chosen, you do not care how you hear about it. Scott was chosen as well and we celebrated at a party he had thrown for his daughter. A week before we were due to leave for South Africa, there was a get-together in Weybridge. The emphasis was on bonding rather than rugby, and it was strange at first because outside of the Wales players, I hardly knew anyone well enough to go up to and strike up a conversation immediately. Players were huddled together according to nationality, though those who had been on previous tours, like Scott Gibbs, Ieuan Evans, Lawrence Dallaglio, and Jason Leonard, did intermingle from the start. It did not take long for the ice to break and the management drew up a rooming list which made sure that no two players from the same country shared. My first room-mate was England full-back Tim Stimpson and throughout the tour I shared with Englishmen – Tony Underwood and Will Greenwood, who both became firm friends of mine, and Neil Back and Nick Beal (the latter two players' names were anagrams of each other, which for some reason always tickled me). Nick and I were to link up a few years later at Northampton.

We had to do a series of exercises at Weybridge after being chosen in different groups: we had to build towers of crates, webs to crawl through and other exercises where you would only succeed if you worked as a team. The management were concerned about the media in South Africa and Peter Jackson, a reporter on the *Daily Mail*, gave us a lecture about what to say and what not to say to reporters. The gameplan was revealed to us, based on continuity with forwards and backs working together, and it was an intense period in terms of the work put in. It had to be. Even though England provided the majority of the players in the squad, the effort in South Africa was going to be four-way and there was no time to lose as far as bonding went. When rugby union turned professional, there were many who sounded the death knell for the Lions because the touring squad was very much an amateur concept, with players going away for months on end in the summer before returning to their clubs worn out and taking three or four months off. The Lions are important financially to South Africa, Australia and New Zealand, and as a player going on one of the tours is the ultimate privilege, but the increasing demands on players are squeezing the Lions.

Before they went to Australia in 2001, players were appearing in top club matches or internationals. There was hardly any warm-up time when the Lions arrived Down Under with just two meaningful matches before the first Test. I far prefer short tours to long ones because too much time away in a regimented and restrictive environment does get to you, but because the Lions only come together every four years, a tour should be two months long. With the club programme expanding all the time and with countries playing more and more internationals to raise money, there is a danger that the Lions could find themselves squeezed out. If that day ever comes, the game all over the world would be immeasurably poorer for it.

While we were at Weybridge, Geech stressed how much we would need to be insular in the sense of sticking together. There would be no one to help us in South Africa and we had to be like a family. We trained with a ball for our last two days there, but with players coming off a long season, the intensity was mental rather than physical that week and the natural competitiveness of players came to the surface. On our last evening, we had a send-off at the Café Royal in London to which wives and girl-friends were not invited (they were there to see us off the next day). We flew out on Virgin with upper-class seats. I had a haircut in the swish lounge we sat around in before boarding the plane. Our first stop was Umhlanga Rocks, a seaside resort on the outskirts of Durban which sounded more exotic than it really was. There had been talk in the media that an alcohol ban had been placed on the players, but that was not the case. Anyone who wanted a drink the night before a match was free to do so; we were all to be judged on our performances in training and in matches. Anyone not looking after himself would be rumbled and either fined or dumped on a plane home.

The players stood to earn £17,000 each if the tour to South Africa was successful, which was measured largely in terms of a series win. The basic pay was £10,000 with an extra £2,000 for one Test victory and £5,000 if we took the best-of-three rubber, though £2,000 hinged on good behaviour. Pro rata, it was not bad pay for a couple of months' work. The value to a player of going with the Lions cannot be measured financially because of the honour involved, but equally there can be no exploitation in the professional age and the percentage of the money generated by the tour which went to the players was not a significant one. In 2001, the maximum earnings went up to £27,000 and in the four years after South Africa, players had become more conscious of their bargaining position. In South Africa, the threat of fines for breaching the code of conduct was always there. There was a senior committee comprising Martin Johnson, Jeremy Guscott, Scott Gibbs, Keith Wood and Lawrence Dallaglio to ensure that players not only behaved responsibly but accepted that by over-indulging or doing anything else to excess they were letting not just themselves down but the rest of the squad and the tour itself.

Tell players that they cannot drink for a night or two before a match and the chances are that someone, indignant at being told what not to do, will. But leave them to their own devices and the bloody-minded, with nothing to object to, react responsibly. It was a clever psychological move – not that any player had gone to South Africa for a party. I like a drink after a match, but only if I feel I have deserved it. There have been times when I have gone home quickly after a victory because I did not think I had played well and was not in the mood for celebration. It is down to the individual, but whereas tours in the amateur days were seen as something in lieu of payment, and a reason to over-indulge at a union's expense too, professionalism is all about results and we returned from South Africa with what we had gone out there for.

My first match was against Border in East London. The much-vaunted dry, hot conditions in South Africa did not come into it – the pitch was a mud-bath and it was like being back in Wales. The ball was soaking, but we kept to our gameplan and did not resort to a kicking game. We won 18–14 and I enjoyed the match. Scott Gibbs's ankle went and he had to leave the field shortly after half-time. There was speculation that he would be the first casualty of the tour, but Paul Grayson had aggravated an old injury and he was actually the first player to be replaced. Scott survived, ready to write his name in rugby history. My second game was much better – with Mpumalanga, who had thrashed Wales in 1995 and drawn with the All Blacks the following year. We beat them soundly, 64–14. We scored ten tries in an awesome display of total rugby which caused some in South

Africa, for the first time, to take us seriously. The only blemish was an appalling foul on Doddie Weir by Marius Bosman which earned the South African a pathetically small fine and no ban. I was meant to play in the next game, against Northern Transvaal, but I tweaked my hamstring in training and had to pull out after pulling up in a run-out the day before the match – which the Lions lost.

The following Wednesday we were playing the Gauteng Lions in Johannesburg and I was told I had to get myself fit for that match. It meant testing the hamstring when rest was needed and aggravating the problem. Scott Quinnell had been injured against Northern Transvaal and his tour was over. I was told that if I did not prove my fitness for Natal on Saturday, the last big match before the first Test the following week, I would be joining him on the flight home. Fran Cotton, the tour manager, told me that it was a case of play or go, and that I would not be carried on the tour. It meant that I found myself in what was otherwise considered to be a shadow Test side against Natal at King's Park. Twelve of the team which started were indeed to play in the first Test and the three unlucky ones were all Welsh. Rob Howley dislocated his shoulder in the first half while David Young and I were both dropped. I came through the Natal match without any problems, but Jerry was chosen ahead of me. I had not had enough time to press my claims, but I still think, looking at the tactics we employed in the first two Tests – with an offensive defence where protecting the gainline was paramount – that I would have been better suited than Jerry. He had been dropped by England that championship, coming on as a replacement on the wing in Cardiff, and it was ironic that as the tour progressed two totally different Lions teams emerged: the Test side was pragmatic and defensive while the midweek team showed flair and imagination. Jerry and I would have been better off swapping places, but I did not feel hard done by because I rated him so highly as a player. Playing second fiddle to him was no disgrace but I felt that the selectors were more afraid of dropping him than they were of picking me.

Natal was the best game I played all tour and our 42–12 victory over one of South Africa's top sides (even if they were without their Springbok squad members) showed that the Test series was not going to be a formality for the home side. Matt Dawson replaced Rob Howley at scrum-half for the first Test while Paul Wallace came in for David Young at tight-head prop. I am not sure why David played against Natal. A hero in Australia in 1989, he had only started one match before Durban. I could not understand why Jim Telfer was so dismissive of him. David, who went on to captain Wales, is invaluable on a tour because of his quick wit and good humour. He did well to retain his optimistic disposition in the face of the way he was treated, something which did no credit to the Lions' management who were otherwise by far and away the best I had worked with. Thoroughly professional and totally dedicated, they left nothing to chance and it is impossible to overstate their role in what was only the Lions' second-ever series victory in South Africa. The fact that McGeechan and Cotton had been players on the other occasion, in 1974, was not a coincidence.

For a reason I never fully understood, the management decided to inform the players and replacements chosen for the first Test by letter, shoved under the doors of our rooms early one morning. I was sharing with Neil Back; he was on the bench while I had the day off. I was not surprised to be missing out, though I thought I had a chance of making the bench, but the disappointment still hit hard. My aim on the tour had been to make the Test side. I had not been content to make the 35 and I felt that I was good enough to be included, but I comforted myself with the thought that I had at least made Jerry work for his place. I also thought I might have been given the week off, but I was chosen to play against the emerging Springboks in the week, a match we won at a canter 51–22.

I watched the first Test from a hospitality box. Those players not involved in the 22 had to do their corporate duty which meant that we got on to the beer long before the players who were to win the match. The Newlands ground in Cape Town was packed and it was virtually impossible to get a programme. The match was nip-and-tuck before Matt Dawson sold the boldest of dummies to put the Lions ahead and Alan Tait finished off. Neil Jenkins kicked superbly and Scott Gibbs put up an heroic display in the centre, tackling with power and conviction. During our first week in South Africa, the hotel we stayed in had a house magazine which contained articles on how the Springboks were going to win the series 3–0 and how we were wasting our time. Suddenly it was game on.

The squad divided in the week between the opening two Tests. The midweek boys flew to Bloemfontein to face Free State while the Test players remained in Durban. Geech did not travel with the dirt-trackers and Telfer was in charge. He gave such an emotional speech before the match that I thought we were going to go out on to the field armed with bayonets. His speech worked and the result was the most complete performance of the tour, a convincing 52–30 victory over opponents who fancied themselves. It provided my one try of the trip but there was a sour note with a serious injury suffered by Will Greenwood who stopped breathing after his head had hit the ground with a sickening thud. He was brought round in the changing rooms, but he was taken to hospital and his tour was over. If I had cause to feel that I was worth a place in the Test side, so did Will, a player who creates space cleverly for others. Neil Jenkins came on to replace him and got a try within a few seconds – so much for his day off after Cape Town!

Next it was back to the hospitality box for the second Test in Durban. The game was not much of a spectacle, but the Lions again played as if their lives depended on the outcome. Scott Gibbs tackled everything that moved and Neil Jenkins kicked every chance he was presented with. Pretty it was not; effective it most certainly was, and Jerry rounded it off with his cool drop-goal at the death.

It was party time that night. I spent most of it with Neil. When he fell into a ditch I had to pull him out, and bundled him into a taxi. We had spent some time in a club behind the ground at King's Park. It was packed with British and Irish supporters and they could not stop mobbing us. One downside for me was that a number of supporters thought I looked like John Bentley, a player who had become a cult-hero on the tour. It was funny at first but then became really annoying. One woman came on to me with her daughters, trying to persuade me to marry one because she thought I was Bentos. The players thought it was hilarious and got the crowd to sing 'There's only one Allan Bateman'. Bentos should have been around with the video camera he always carried with him. He once claimed to have caught a player in a compromising position having sneaked into his room with some magazines. The camera rolled, Bentos laughed and shot out of the room as the unfortunate player realised what had happened. Bentos dropped the camera in his own room before going downstairs to tell the rest of the squad what he had captured for eternity. There were howls of disbelief and Bentos was ordered to get his camera and provide proof. He came down, set it to play and there was nothing. It turned out that the player concerned had climbed on to the balcony (risking a considerable drop to the ground in the process), made his way to Bentos's room and erased the film.

We spent the final week at a place called Vanderbijl Park on the outskirts of Johannesburg. It may have been someone's idea of a good time, but it was no sort of reward for winning the series. It was a dump. The rooms were freezing and morale fell through the floor as a number of players went down with a gastric bug. The final midweek match was against Northern Free State, a team expected to provide no more than token opposition. We won 67–39 but we conceded a couple of late tries, and the management tore into us. They said it had been the most disappointing performance of the tour and that the way we had let them come back had been disgraceful. It was a pointless show of power – words for words' sake, and even Geech joined in. I do not know if it was intended to galvanise the players for the third Test when only the Springboks had something to play for, but whatever the method was behind the madness, it failed miserably. It was one of the few occasions when the management made a serious misjudgement. We ended the tour unbeaten in midweek, though, and we had played some superb rugby. The players who had not made the Test team had not allowed their heads or their performances to drop. Considering that Geech had been in charge in New Zealand in 1993 when the midweek team did perform disgracefully, thrashed by Hawke's Bay and Waikato, I thought he would have reacted differently. Yes, we had conceded a couple of soft tries when the match had long been won, but it was nothing to get overheated about.

I did not get to know Geech well personally on the tour, but on a professional basis I found him excellent to work with. He did not bark at players, unlike Telfer, but he had a firm idea of what he wanted. The two of them together made for a 'good cop–bad cop' partnership but Geech was straight and left you in no confusion about what he wanted. He was the best coach I had experienced and the only one who rivals him in my career is Graham Henry, who took over the Wales squad in August 1998. Geech is straighter than Henry, but they both have radical ideas. I did not agree with the decision to appoint Henry as the Lions' coach for the 2001 Australia tour, not because he was not up to the job, far from it, but because he was not British or Irish. Nationality is important to me at international level, and I disagreed with Henry when he introduced foreigners into the Wales squad soon after his arrival. I could understand his thinking, but you should not pick and choose when it comes to a country and it was a natural justice of sorts when Henry found himself caught up in an eligibility scandal during the 2000 Six Nations.

I had been given the nod by a member of the management that I would play in the third Test, with Jerry moved to the wing, but when I got my letter under the door I found that I was on the bench. Because I had only been told of my selection unofficially, there was no way I could complain and I have never really found out what happened. In his book on the tour, Geech said that while he felt I deserved to play and that he had toyed with the idea of playing Jerry on the wing, he was concerned that there would be too many changes with a number of players, including Keith Wood, Alan Tait and Gregor Townsend, struggling with injuries. I spoke to the person on the management who had congratulated me on my selection and all he could say was: 'Yesterday you were playing.'

I got my chance to play when Jerry broke his arm at half-time and I won my Lions cap, but it would have meant more had I been chosen on merit. I made one mistake which cost us a try: Neil did not follow a move through and I ended up holding on to the ball for too long. It is always hard coming on as a replacement because you cannot get the feel of a game instantly and there is always the danger that you try too hard to make an impact. I went on to make a try-saving tackle, but it was a match too far for the Lions and we lost 35–16 after the Springboks pulled away in the final quarter. We still celebrated that night and into the following day, though I saw no evidence of the alleged recreational drug-taking by some players that ended up plastered in a newspaper two years after the tour. One thing that had surprised me in South Africa was an absence of drug-testing despite all that the International Rugby Board was saying about providing an effective deterrent should anyone be tempted to take banned substances. I would be amazed, though, if anyone in the squad had taken any sort of drugs during the tour because of the family bond which had been generated. No one would have taken the risk of chucking everything away, surely.

It was the greatest experience of my rugby career and a tour which captured the imagination of sports followers in Britain and Ireland, creating a feel-good factor which the clubs profited from the following winter. Nicola had been unable to come out for any part of it because of her job in a department store in Oxford Street which she had only just started. It took me a long time to get over the tour, not so much physically but mentally. I do not think I spoke to Nicola properly for three months afterwards. I had been part of a rigid framework for two months that revolved around training, eating, sleeping and playing with no distractions. Everything was laid on for you and suddenly I found myself at home where there was nothing organised for you. I suppose it was like coming out of the armed services: you have a lot of time on your hands and there is no one giving you orders. I felt lost. It had been only the second tour of my career after Namibia in 1990 and it took a lot out of me. Not that I would not do it all again – more's the pity that, after being overlooked in 2001, I know that I will never have the chance again. I have the memories, and they will last me a lifetime.

ELEVEN

HENRY THE FIRST

Few in Wales had heard of Graham Henry when he took over from Kevin Bowring as the national coach in August 1998. The fortunes of the national side were at their lowest ebb. The record defeats against England and France earlier in the year had been overshadowed by a 96–13 defeat against South Africa in Pretoria that June. It was far from a full-strength Wales team that played, with the bulk of the players who had appeared in the Five Nations unable to tour for various reasons, but only a knock-on denied the Springboks their century of points in what had been the most humiliating scoreline in the history of any of the major rugby nations. Grand Slam winners in 1978 and only a controversial penalty away from beating the All Blacks that year, Wales had become a laughing stock and the Welsh Rugby Union decided that the answer to their prayers no longer lay within.

Henry was the coach of Auckland, Auckland Blues and New Zealand A with a record second to none below full international level. Wales had never had a full-time coach from overseas before. Alex Evans, an Australian, had been in charge of Wales during the World Cup on a caretaker basis, but the WRU decided to trawl the world after their shocking results in 1998 and Henry, who had been approached by England the previous year, was offered an annual salary of £250,000 and a five-year contract. In one sense, it was a bold move, admitting that the problems facing Welsh rugby demanded the presence of someone from outside, but in another it reinforced the tendency of the Union to look to an individual for salvation rather than making sweeping changes to the structure of the game. They got more than they bargained for with Henry. When he arrived, Cardiff and Swansea pulled out of the Welsh league to play unsanctioned friendlies against the leading English clubs and he wasted no time in getting involved on the political side. Henry quickly sensed the strong position he was in: the WRU had admitted that he was their last chance and the New Zealander was not going to waste any opportunity to exploit that to the full. He was able to get away with acts that Bowring would have been reprimanded for at the very least, such as ignoring Union advice not to watch Cardiff and Swansea (and so be seen to be supporting the rebels). He commanded more authority in the corridors of power than his predecessors and David Pickering, the former Wales captain who was a member of the Welsh Rugby Union's general committee, was appointed the manager of the Wales squad.

Henry quickly mended the fences with Richmond. He got rid of the divisive contract system and replaced it with one based on appearances – the more caps you had won, the more you were paid – but the system had to be revised because Henry's consistency in selection meant that players were piling up the caps and a ceiling was eventually put on 40 caps. He turned up more than occasionally to our matches and even our training sessions. At the start of his time with Wales, the Quinnell brothers, Barry Williams and I were in the Wales squad while John Davies had played the Test match in South Africa. Henry reasoned that as so many of his players were at the club, he had to pay it more than cursory attention but at our first meeting with him he made it plain that he wanted us to return to Wales, and not just to any old club. His vision of the future was that only four or five professional sides would be sustainable in Wales and within a few months Scott Quinnell, for personal reasons, moved back to Llanelli. Henry specified which clubs were worth joining. I pointed out that Newport had come in for me but that as they were not in the Heineken Cup I was not interested. This was not the whole truth – I did not want to return to Wales with the club scene there in turmoil. I knew that Northampton had shown an interest in me but

Richmond were then in a sound financial position and were unwilling to release me. It was the only time that I have had more than a brief conversation with Henry. Players find it easy to banter with him, but not to talk on a one-to-one basis. When you are dropped or substituted, he never gives an explanation. The first you know is when the side is read out at a team meeting or when you are put in formation at the first training session before a match. Kevin Bowring was totally different, going out of his way to provide explanations, but you have to ask Henry and that is hardly encouraged.

As a coach, he is as good as anyone I have worked with. His track record in New Zealand was phenomenal and he boasted a success rate of more than 80 per cent. He had always harboured ambitions of coaching the All Blacks but when he accepted the WRU's offer, John Hart looked secure as New Zealand's coach (a position which was to change within a few months). Henry wanted to coach an international side and Wales gave him the opportunity, but it was a big step for him to take, not just coming to a foreign country, but resuscitating the sick man of world rugby at a time when civil war was breaking out.

Henry's first game in charge was, ironically, South Africa at Wembley. I missed the match through injury and the international against Argentina at Llanelli later in the month too. Henry immediately changed all the moves and he changed our style which had been deep and wide under Bowring to one which was flat and narrow. It did not suit me because my strength is in going on the outside and that means running on to the ball rather than taking it virtually standing still – but I was willing to give it a go. In many regards, he was always willing to try something new and he listened when players made points in team meetings or on the training field. He never left anyone in any doubt who was in charge, but he rarely betrayed the fact that he had been a teacher before becoming a full-time coach. He treated players as equals and never spoke down to them. He commanded respect and loyalty and it was quickly clear that he had not come to Wales to sacrifice his reputation.

He did not jump in with a welter of pre-conceived ideas and he stuck largely to the squad he inherited. Rob Howley remained captain and when David Young and I had recovered from our injuries, we were immediately selected in the side for the start of the 1999 Five Nations Championship. Henry had clearly been given a lot of advice in his first few weeks in Wales, but he wanted to see everything for himself. Whether someone did or did not rate a player was not good enough for him. He had to make up his own mind and some players who had been tipped for the scrapheap (Neil Jenkins for example) enjoyed not only a new lease of life but played with an authority and a freedom that did Henry credit. Players had never doubted Neil's ability and competitiveness, but he had always been messed around in his career, moved to centre and full-back and occasionally dropped. Henry was the first coach who told him that he was his leading outside-half and to get on with it. It meant Neil did not have to look over his shoulder and it showed the difference Henry made: he was adept at taking pressure off players and absorbing it himself. His position allowed that, but he saw virtues in Neil that others had missed and the results spoke for themselves.

The other side of the coin was that once Henry had a downer on a player, it took a lot to change his mind. The Swansea wing Matthew Robinson was chosen at the start of the 1999 championship and had a couple of decent games before being substituted in Paris. He was taken on the summer tour to Argentina where he played in the first Test, but he was then left out of the World Cup squad and has hardly figured since. Arwel Thomas also had a long time in the wilderness before being given his chance under Henry while the likes of Chris Wyatt and Peter Rogers, who had at one stage looked certainties to make the Lions tour of South Africa in 2001, failed to even make the Wales squad that went to Japan that summer. Dafydd James was dropped after the international against France in 2000 and his international career looked to be over, but he bounced back on the strength of his performances for Llanelli. There was a period when Dafydd seemed to be the odd man out: his would always be the name left off the rooming list. When Graham was showing videos and asking for players' observations he would agree with everyone but Dafydd, and he generally seemed to be ignored. I raised the matter with Trevor James, the squad administrator, and he said the snubs were not deliberate. Dafydd became involved from that instant. Henry is very much a form man and he likes players to be mentally strong, which is why he likes to give emerging players time to establish themselves in senior rugby before chucking them into the international pool. He is concerned at the effect the media can have on players: the 'tall poppy syndrome' as some call it. Players react differently to criticism, but it is a myth to say that no one reads newspapers. They are pounced on avidly, not least because they are a great source for mickey-taking if someone has said something inane or outrageous – but harsh words can gnaw away at players like a cancer and Henry, surprised at the depth of the coverage of the game in Wales, and its fanaticism, has tended to wait before blooding players rather than risk seeing them destroyed for good by a media battering.

I have never been bothered by what is said about me in the media, but I have been fortunate that no one has ever had a major go at me – or at least not that I am aware of. I have never been a 'tall poppy' and I have been allowed to do my own thing. When I am interviewed, I always say what I think; there is no point in answering questions unless you are prepared to tell the truth, but it is one of sport's anomalies that there are some players who can get away with things while others are panned for stepping ever so slightly out of line. Rugby is the national sport of Wales, at least in the south of the country, and it follows that there will be in-depth coverage in the print and broadcast media. In the end, though, it is only words, tomorrow's fish-and-chip paper. Life goes on.

Henry had a long honeymoon even though three of his first four matches ended in defeat. The first time he came under any sustained pressure was in March 2000 when the Grannygate affair broke. Henry had turned to players outside Wales immediately after taking charge. Shane Howarth, the former New Zealand international who was playing for Sale, was drafted into the side immediately while the Neath flanker Brett Sinkinson, another New Zealander, was brought in after the poor start. Peter Rogers, a prop who was born in Kent and raised in Wales before emigrating to South Africa, made his debut along with Sinkinson. That summer, just before the start of the World Cup, the centre Jason Jones-Hughes, who had a Welsh father, was brought over from Australia having been chosen for the squad for the tournament. Andy Marinos was placed on a national contract after being lured from South Africa.

Howarth and Sinkinson claimed to have Welsh grandparents, but it emerged that the WRU had not even made a cursory effort to establish these claims as facts and that the pair had played despite being ineligible to wear the Wales jersey. Howarth was only rumbled after 19 appearances and the affair may not have come to light, ironically, but for the recruitment of Jason Jones-Hughes. Australia protested to the International Rugby Board that, while Jones-Hughes may have been qualified to play for Wales through his father, as he had played for Australia A he had, under the rules, committed himself to Australia for life. The Board initially ruled in the Australian Rugby Union's favour but then found for Jones-Hughes on appeal and he was allowed to take his place in Wales's World Cup squad.

The protracted wrangle made an issue of eligibility and the media started digging into the backgrounds of Howarth and Sinkinson. After Wales had lost heavily at Twickenham in 1999, a newspaper claimed to have proof that the pair had no right to play for Wales. The story broke as the Wales squad was gathering for the international against Scotland in Cardiff. Sinkinson never appeared, but Howarth, who had proclaimed his eligibility to play for Wales before Henry's arrival, turned up and he was, according to the grapevine, chosen to play at outside-half in place of the injured Neil Jenkins. The WRU, forced to take action, demanded that Howarth provide his grandfather's birth certificate before being allowed to take his place in the side. The next Monday he left the hotel and has not played for Wales since.

The players were initially suspicious of both Howarth and Sinkinson, but we assumed their claims had been checked out and authenticated. There was never any question about their value to Wales. They were both significant additions to the team, but when they were rumbled I did not feel any sympathy for them. A country is not like a club and the effect of Jones-Hughes incident was the transfer of a player from Australia to Wales at a significant cost even though he was unproven at international level. Henry went further and tried to arrange bursaries for South African students in Wales so that by the time they had completed their studies, they would have lived in Wales for three years and so qualified to play for their new country on residential grounds. Were we really that bad in Wales? Appointing coaches from overseas is one thing, but a line has to be drawn when it comes to players and centre was one position where Wales had strength in depth. What were Jones-Hughes and Marinos going to bring to the team? If they had been players of the highest quality, they would already have been capped.

The question the media were asking was whether Henry knew that Howarth and Sinkinson were ineligible. Had he chosen them in blatant disregard for the rules? The Board set up an inquiry panel which banned the players but did little more than rap the WRU over the knuckles for not checking out the players' claims to have had Welsh grandparents. The system was deemed to be at fault rather than individuals and the only two who ended up being punished were Howarth and Sinkinson which seemed wrong to me because they had only done what they had been asked to do. Henry was without question worried. The players had nicknamed him 'Scrunchy' because of his contorted facial expressions, especially when he was making a joke – but there was no smiling in the build-up to the Scotland game. The glint in his eye and the smirk on his face had gone and he made far fewer quips to the players. Whether Henry knew what had been going on or not only he can answer, but he was without question stained by the affair and it took him a while to recover his old poise.

I felt sorry for the players who had missed out because of Howarth and Sinkinson. One of them, Byron Hayward, made a public attack on Henry and said that he was not prepared to play for any Wales side again while Henry was still in charge. Byron was then playing for Gloucester and his remarks were printed in a local paper there. When I spoke to him later, he said that he had meant his criticism of Henry but had not gone so far as to say he would never play for his country again. It was a sorry affair which did Welsh rugby no credit, but Henry survived and within a few months was appointed coach for the Lions tour to Australia in the summer of 2001.

Until the eligibility storm broke, Henry had enjoyed an easy ride. His first game in charge saw Wales come within eight minutes of their first ever victory over South Africa. Wales took a 14-point lead at Wembley and took the game to the team which had nearly scored 100 points against them five months previously. South Africa pulled away at the end, but the reaction in Wales was that the saviour had arrived and Graham Henry became known as 'the Redeemer'. Victory followed against Argentina (though not before their pack had handed out a scrummaging lesson) and then it was time to prepare for what was to be the last ever Five Nations Championship, with Italy due to enter the tournament from 2000.

Our opening match was in Scotland, as it had been in 1997. The 'Henry factor' meant that Wales were made firm favourites to win. I was recalled at outside-centre in place of Mark Taylor who had played well against both South Africa and Argentina. Henry had not had much of a look at me, but I had been the man in possession before he arrived and he wanted to make his own mind up. It was the last time I was chosen ahead of Mark on form. Scotland had a dream start when John Leslie, one of their New Zealand recruits, scored a try from the kick-off, but we took control until Gregor Townsend scored an interception try in the second half and we ended up losing a match we should have won comfortably. Henry was taken aback by the occasion. The championship was often ridiculed in the southern hemisphere for the quality of rugby it generated, but what television there failed to bring across was that a championship weekend is not just about the rugby. When Henry looked out of his hotel window on Saturday morning and saw thousands of supporters in red scarves, he thought his eyes were playing up and in that moment he understood the emotion which courses through the veins of rugby followers in Wales.

It was the first time I had played under Henry's new flat back line system. I had an ordinary match, dropping off a couple of tackles, and my lack of size told against me. Unable to run on to the ball, the flat line meant that strength was more important than speed and Mark had an advantage over me because he was taller and heavier, better suited to riding through tacklers.

I do not know whether Henry would have stuck with me for the Ireland international because I strained my hamstring playing for Richmond against Sale and had to pull out again. We had hoped that the curse of the Irish in Cardiff would not travel as far as Wembley, but it did and we lost despite making a fight back in the second half. It meant our two final matches were against France, who were looking for a third successive Grand Slam – and England, who were the championship favourites. We were strongly fancied to record our third whitewash in eight years.

The game against France in Paris was where it all really started for Henry. I had been chosen on the bench and was taking part in the team run out at the Stade de France when I felt a pain in my calf. Within a few minutes I could not walk. I had to be carried from the field and Gareth Thomas was called up from the A team to take my place on the bench. The injury ruled me out for the rest of the international season and at the time I thought my international career had come to an anti-climactic end. To sit in the stand in Paris that Saturday was to witness one of the most incredible international matches I had ever seen. Wales had brought in Sinkinson, Rogers and Garin Jenkins at forward and the game was taken to France from the kick-off. There was no time to draw breath in the first half with both sides running from deep. Wales's last victory in Paris had been in 1975 and no one had been backing us to end our run of defeats in the French capital.

This was one of those days when things came off. We surprised France with our tactical approach. They had been expecting what they called 'boring British rugby', and when Neil Jenkins ran from under his own posts in the opening minute, it was as if someone had caught them out with an April Fool. France could still have won though. Thomas Castaignède, the hero at Wembley the year before, had a penalty to win the match in the final minute but it drifted inches wide; the small margin between success and failure. It was party time. I wanted to be on my own having missed out on the success. When I am not playing, I am as keen on Wales winning as any supporter, but after the post-match dinner I just felt like going back to the hotel. The players carried me on to the coach, though, and most of the rest of the night is a blur.

Wales then overwhelmed Italy in Rome before the final match of the Five Nations against England at Wembley. Victory would give the English the Grand Slam and the title, while a Wales win would see Scotland crowned champions. I saw the match on a big screen at the London Welsh club and had arranged to meet the players at their hotel that evening with Nicola. I could not face going to Wembley having been ruled out of the match by injury. Nicola could not get away because of work though, and the players were, not surprisingly, late after another amazing victory. England looked to have been in the box seat all match, but a late Scott Gibbs try and a Neil Jenkins conversion ensured that Henry was given the freedom of Wales: the redeemer indeed. I decided not to wait; it was their celebration, not mine, and I drove home.

The sequence of results in 1999 was the start of a trend. In 2000, we lost to France and England, defeating Italy in between, before winning our final two matches and in 2001, we lost to England and drew in Scotland before finishing with two victories. It is hard to explain why we started slowly and finished strongly under Graham Henry and several reasons have been thrown up. There is no obvious explanation – but it is when the pressure is on and we most have to deliver, as it was in 1999 against Scotland after the eligibility crisis, that we tend to come good. The Scots fancied their chances that day. We were rocking anyway after the 46–12 defeat at Twickenham and Henry had to blood some new players: Stephen Jones came in at outside-half, Matt Cardey replaced Howarth at full-back, Nathan Budgett was chosen in the back row while Ian Gough and Andy Moore formed a new pairing in the second row.

I was playing at inside-centre with Mark Taylor as I had against Italy and England that championship. I had first played there on the 1999 summer tour to Argentina. Scott Gibbs had pulled out with an injury and Henry wanted to see how Mark and I would go together. I had never played at inside-centre. I had played left and right with Leigh Davies for Wales and I was comfortable with that but for someone who liked to find space on the outside, inside-centre for me was claustrophobic. Henry told Mark and I to sort it out between us where we played. He did not fancy inside-centre at all and he was not comfortable with the idea of left and right so I ended up replacing Scott – in person but not in kind. The first 20 minutes of the first Test in Argentina were distinctly uncomfortable, not just because they took a healthy early lead but because I did not know where I was. Props go on about the difference between loose-head and tight-head and it is the same with the centre positions. You see more of the ball at inside-centre, but you are operating in a tight channel where contact is unavoidable and I prefer to have more time to weigh up options.

Scott missed the June 1999 international against South Africa at the Millennium Stadium, my finest hour in a Wales jersey. It was the first match at the ground, which was still being completed and which only had a capacity of 25,000. It was the first time we had beaten South Africa. We scored two well-worked tries and defended like demons. The Springboks were not at full strength, but the previous year they had equalled New Zealand's record for the most consecutive number of Test matches without defeat and they had just put 100 points on Italy. It was almost a year to the day after Pretoria and that 13–96 was turned into 29–19. Henry had played down publicly our chances of winning, saying it was a match too far and that he would rather the game not be played, but that was not what he told the players. We had kept a winning run going in Argentina and South Africa were seen as a key stepping-stone to the World Cup. Neil Jenkins, the scourge of South Africa in 1997, was at it again with seven successful kicks out of eight and it made for one of the biggest days in Wales's history.

That day marked the high point under Henry. Winning raised expectations. I did not celebrate that night because I did not think I played that well. I am self-critical and to me a beer after a game has to be earned. I stayed on the soft stuff and drove back to London that night. Henry became more than a national hero. When we toured around Wales before the World Cup, it was as if some supporters really felt that he had divine qualities and that he could turn water into wine. He had turned things round, without question, but suddenly we had become potential World Cup winners in the eyes of some – and however hard Henry tried to play down expectation, our results only served to increase it. He proved far more adept than any of his predecessors at using the media, always managing to get his message across.

The newspapers gave the players the best clue as to what he was thinking. You never really knew with him. He did not shout and bawl, but nor did he sit you down and talk things through. When you did speak to him, or when he was addressing a team meeting, his eyes never gave him away. He could have been saying one thing but meaning another; you would not know. It was unnerving, but we all had faith in him. He knew how to get the best out of players and he constantly changed things on the coaching front. At times he was derivative. After Australia won the World Cup in 1999, he took a lot of their ideas on board and after we were thrashed in Cardiff by England in 2001, he used some of their ideas too. It was the sign of a good coach – never afraid to change direction and never arrogant enough to think that you know it all. But it was clear a couple of years into his reign that one man had not simply arrived in Wales with a magic wand and one question remained unanswered: what would happen after Henry returned to New Zealand following the 2003 World Cup?

Henry was always one for surprises. He dropped Rob Howley as captain after the 1999 World Cup without giving a firm reason, even to Rob. Within a couple of games, Rob had lost his place at scrum-half even though he was, by some distance, the best player in the position in Wales. Yet within six months, he was not only back in the Wales side but also playing some of the best rugby of his career. No one could figure out Henry's reasoning at the time, but it worked. It was if he was able to see ahead into the future.

There are other times when players simply cannot understand him. When we played Scotland at Murrayfield in 2001. Stephen Jones had been chosen at full-back but he ricked his back in the week of the game and there was a doubt whether he would play. Henry had told Stephen that if he had to pull out it would mean Gareth Thomas or me being moved from the bench and dropped into the A squad because he needed to call on a specialist full-back. Nothing wrong with the rugby reasoning there, but Henry did not tell Gareth ('Alfie') or me. When Stephen was forced to pull out on the Friday morning, Henry came up to Alfie at breakfast and told him to pack his bags and join the A squad who were playing that night. Alfie, who had had some run-ins with Henry over lifestyle, went to reception and checked out without arguing the decision, but it was clear he was burning inside, and he and I should have been forewarned.

Alfie came on in the second half in the A game and he enjoyed himself in Edinburgh that night. He went to a few pubs and wound up supporters who asked him what he was doing drinking the night before an international. They were unaware that he had been pulled out of the 22, and he led them on something rotten. I have a lot of time for Alfie. He has never had a bad game for Wales, and even if he does like a drink and a smoke, nothing gets in the way of his rugby. He was left out of one of the autumn internationals after being seen the worse for wear in Cardiff following a Heineken Cup victory over Toulouse, but he is a player I would always have in my side and I was surprised when he was left out of the 2001 Lions tour to Australia.

Henry does lose patience with players. Chris Wyatt, a naturally talented second-row, is another player who likes to relax. Henry got a lot out of Chris in his first 18 months, but he wearied of the player's lifestyle. That in itself would not have been enough to see Chris thrown out of the squad, but when his performances on the pitch dropped, his conduct became a factor. Henry set standards, but he is not the schoolmasterly type and players are given latitude. The proof is seen as in the playing and if you let yourself down, he lets you go.

TWELVE

ANOTHER WORLD

The 1999 rugby union World Cup was totally different from the 1995 rugby league tournament which turned out to be a farewell party. The eyes of the world were on Cardiff and the new Millennium Stadium. Optimism was in the air after a run of eight consecutive victories by Wales and we had an enviable draw with Argentina, Japan and Samoa making up our group. It put us on a collision course for Australia in the quarter-finals if we both finished top of our pools, but we would have home advantage. At the start of the competition, we could not afford to look ahead to the quarter-finals, having failed to reach the last eight in both 1991 and 1995, but our preparation had been thorough and morale could not have been higher.

One of Graham Henry's first appointments was the conditioning coach Steve Black, a larger-than-life Geordie who had worked with Newcastle United and the Newcastle rugby club after a career which had taken in boxing and powerlifting, among other sports. Blackie made it plain he did not want to be known as a fitness coach with all the testing that the title implied. His predecessor had been a South African, Dave Clark, who had worked in a health and racquets club. He was very much into logging, timing and measuring, treating the players as a group and never bringing a personal touch to his work. He tested players for speed and strength rather than working with them. He was good at what he did as far as it went, but he did not extend himself or the members of the squad.

Not only was Blackie's approach completely different because testing was a foreign concept to him, but he became a father-figure to many players, available at all hours for them. His infectious enthusiasm, unquenchable optimism and permanent smile were invaluable in helping lift the battered morale of players. He did not like testing players because he did not believe that the results meant much; he preferred to make up his own mind about a player's condition and believed that fitness was made up of the mental as well as the physical element. Some players came to swear by him and a number still get him to draw up their fitness schedules. As I was based in England and as Henry abandoned the weekly national squad sessions which Kevin Bowring had organised, I only saw Blackie in the build-up to matches.

I could see where Blackie was coming from, but I did not subscribe totally to his methods. He resigned during the 2000 Six Nations and his replacement, Peter Herbert, was a mixture of Blackie and Dave Clark and of the three coaches he suited me best. One of the reasons I continued playing at an age when most players had retired was that I had always done a lot of endurance work on my own. Peter Herbert subscribed to the testing method, but he did not see everything measured in terms of results. When it comes to fitness, there have to be tests to provide a coach with a measure of where a player is. Blackie gave up his job after a sustained campaign in the media against the perceived lack of fitness among the Wales players, a bandwagon which gathered momentum after the 46–12 defeat against England at Twickenham. Blackie was pilloried for relying on quack methods, so the arguments went, and for not being scientific enough. If the accusers had a point (which I did not accept), they were pointing their arrows in the wrong direction. Between the end of the World Cup and the start of the Six Nations, Blackie had not seen the players. If there was a problem with their fitness, the responsibility was the fitness coaches' at club level and even then the criticism would have been unfair because club rugby is totally different from the international scene. What passes as fit in the former would not do so in the latter. It amounted to a typically Welsh search for scapegoats. As someone whose smile was not only his trademark but also his business card, Blackie felt that the more the pressure built on him from the outside, the less he would be able to do his job properly and his exit, at the time that the Grannygate affair blew up, could not have been less timely. He was the perfect foil for Graham Henry, a more serious man who lacked Blackie's spontaneity. It was much quieter without our conditioning coach.

One problem in the game since professionalism has been the overloading of players, not merely in terms of the fixture list but more in training schedules. At Richmond one summer, we went on a pre-season tour to Ireland where we had a couple of games. I felt that we were doing too much and said so at a meeting when the coaches asked for comments from the players. John Kingston exploded and said: 'You are paid to play and you will do what I tell you.' It was an unthinking response. There comes a point when the harder you flog players, the less you get out of them. Blackie realised that and the fact that Wales enjoyed their best run for more than 90 years while he was with us – along with the trophies won by Newcastle during his time there before and after Wales, proved the importance of ensuring that players were mentally sharp and not just at their peak physically.

Blackie suffered from sleep apnoea, a dangerous condition which meant that he had to wear an oxygen mask when he slept because he could stop breathing. He would often be up for most of the night and would fall asleep during the day. Graham Henry would be talking to him or delivering a state-of-the-nation speech to the players and Blackie, standing up, would have nodded off. His essential strength was in mixing things up. He recognised that international players were physically fit, but they were not always mentally stimulated. The rugby environment can be mind-numbingly boring: training, sitting around in hotels watching rubbish on television, eating boring food and sticking to a school-like timetable. Blackie was conscious of laughter's therapeutic value. He would often come into the team-room and fall on the floor, like a character in a slapstick comedy. When we went to the cinema the night before an international, he would walk into a glass door or pretend to faint. When he resigned, it was left to Rupert Moon and me to lift team morale. As two of the elder statesmen, we were not put on any of the sub-committees that related to playing strategy because of our age. Rupert had not played for Wales for five years when Henry recalled him to replace Rob

131

Howley, and like Blackie he was a character who permanently bubbled.

Blackie's preparation for the World Cup started in the summer of 1999 when we toured Argentina. I knew two of their players, Agustin Pichot and Rolando Martin, from Richmond and they warned me how tough it was going to be: no side had achieved a whitewash in a Test series there and when we lost our first match against Buenos Aires we were looking down the barrel. It got even worse at the start of the first Test when we trailed by 23 points in as many minutes. I was playing out of position at inside-centre while Neil Jenkins was making his first appearance for a couple of months after an operation. We looked rusty, but our forwards took charge and we staged probably the most remarkable comeback I had experienced in my career, winning 36–26. I swapped shirts with Pichot after the match and he was disgusted with the way his side had collapsed. The second Test was played the following week and we never looked like losing it. Play was interrupted for a while after a punch-up which involved some cameramen and occupants of a dug-out. I have never quite understood why players get involved in brawls. That incident had started when one of their players had set upon our wing Dafydd James and the next thing you knew, most of the players were trading punches (though precious few connected). There is safety in numbers as far as making it difficult for a referee to send someone off is concerned, but some players cannot resist niggling. Jonathan Davies may have been an outside-half, but he knew how to wind up opponents. We were in the same side for a Warrington against St Helens match and Jonathan started fighting with an opponent. He was not one who took particular care about where his elbows went and often encouraged acts of retaliation. He was so important to Warrington that as soon as I saw him fighting, I went to pull the other guy away. I had him pinned and Jonathan took the opportunity to land a few more blows. I was shouting at him to stop otherwise he would be sent off, but he got away with it – as he always seemed to.

The Argentina tour confirmed our revival and gave us an important psychological advantage because we were facing the Pumas in the opening match of the World Cup at the Millennium Stadium that October. We knew that we would have to play well below ourselves to lose that match and by the time we left Argentina for home, the perception of Wales, both inside the squad and outside, was in total contrast to what it had been less than a year before. None of the players who had gone to Argentina returned home injured, a first for a country which had gained a reputation for being bad tourists. Blackie had a lot to do with that. Even though we were made very welcome, conditions there were not the best. Our first hotel was the Hindu Club on the outskirts of Buenos Aires – quaint but dated. There was nothing to do for us there and on one of the days a bus trip was organised to a major carnival. We ended up visiting Eva Peron's grave. The bus driver got lost when we travelled to the ground for the first Test, a promised police escort had failed to materialise, but fortunately we had left in plenty of time.

We travelled by coach from Buenos Aires to Rosario for the match against Argentina A, a six-hour drive. On the way back, the bus we were travelling in, which looked as if it had been built before even I was born, kept overheating and the driver had to stop every so often to let the engine cool down before filling up the radiator. Some players passed the time by indulging in gambling, playing three-card brag for money. The stakes grew increasingly high, reaching the point where it was not a case of cash on the table but IOUs. You were talking thousands of pounds and some players ended up losing more than their tour fees. There were six to eight players in the school and one of them, after losing a considerable sum of money, claimed that he was not in a state to pay up, after losing his wallet in a nearby McDonalds (a story that smacked of convenience – there was no way he was getting out of paying up). Graham Henry found out about the sums of money which were being bet and launched a clampdown. IOUs were outlawed and players had to play for petty cash only.

I was never tempted to join in. Your money is too hard-earned to be thrown away, and there had been a crackdown on players gambling on rugby after various rumours and allegations. Cricket was rife with match-fixing speculation and Mark Ring, the former Cardiff and Wales centre, claimed a couple of years ago that he had been offered £30,000 by an anonymous caller to throw the match between Wales and Ireland in Dublin in 1990. I am not sure that many believed Ringo; Wales lost so many matches in those days that no one needed to offer pay as an incentive, but Ringo was telling the truth. It was my second match for Wales and, before we left for Ireland, we stayed at the Angel Hotel in Cardiff. A well known figure in Welsh rugby asked me if I would be interested in £5,000 to help ensure that Wales lost. I turned him down flat, but I worried about it for days afterwards. Did this sort of thing go on all the time? Or was it a test? Perhaps there was no offer, merely a temptation to see how I would react. It was a bizarre experience. It was never mentioned again after I had said no and I never spoke about it to anyone.

The Wales card school was essentially a vehicle to relieve boredom, even if it did get out of hand, but I have never come across players betting on their team to lose. There was a bookmakers on the ground at Northampton and some players would often put a couple of quid on themselves to score the first try and I have known occasions in the past where players put money on the other team – but only when their side had been given 30 or 40 points start. That is a grey area, someone betting on the other team, but it does not involve his own side losing. If one team is given a 45-point start, for instance, a 44–0 defeat would see the other side 'winning' as far as the bookies are concerned. So although your own team has won the match, you would clear up because the margin of victory was not 45 points. The International Rugby Board issued an edict saying that anyone involved in the game, from players down to kit men, was not allowed to bet on rugby, whether they were involved in a match or not. There was not a problem, certainly not in Wales or England, but it made sense to lay down the law. The game has to be seen to be above any shadiness.

After Argentina, we had a few days off before preparing for South Africa at the Millennium Stadium and then we had a month's holiday before the countdown to the World Cup started in earnest. Blackie arranged a programme for us which took in the whole of Wales and ended in the sunshine of Portugal. We started in the Brecon Beacons and we moved on to North Wales and Pembrokeshire. The new environments added a freshness to the routines and we did different kinds of fitness work in the various locations. That summer, starting on tour, was the only time Blackie had the players for any length of time and there were no question marks placed over our fitness. I felt that the main drawback of his method was that because he did not see the players regularly during the season (apart from Craig Quinnell who had a clause inserted into his contract with Cardiff which allowed him to do his fitness work with Blackie) he therefore had no definite idea of what shape they were in. Blackie was appointed the conditioning coach for the Lions tour to Australia in 2001 and that is the ideal environment for him. Over a longer period, you needed more structure and planning, but his part in Wales's initial revival under Graham Henry should not be understated. He had radical ideas, but he made players feel confident, telling them that they were the best in the world and getting them to believe that. As a motivator, he was the best I had come across, a remarkable man who had the misfortune to discover that in Wales there are always some who are jealous of success.

We had two capped warm-up matches before the start of the World Cup: Canada and France at the Millennium Stadium, and there was also a friendly against the United States. I was chosen on the left wing against Canada. This was my first experience in the position in rugby union since my days with Maesteg. When I was interviewed by reporters about the move, I said that I loathed the position and there were various headlines the following day highlighting my feelings. Graham Henry did not say anything to me, but from then on I did not mention the subject. After I had scored three tries against the United States on the left wing, he merely came up to me and said: 'Not bad for someone who does not like playing on the wing.' I had spoken out because of how I remembered the position in the 1980s: lonely and isolated with little to do for the most part. I had not appreciated how much the role of a wing had changed. There was far more involvement and you were expected to go looking for the ball. I was pleasantly surprised and the position no longer disconcerts me.

We defeated Canada 33–19, with Neil Jenkins scoring 28 points, and I then sat out the 34–23 victory over France. I had been assured of a place in the World Cup squad after the victory over South Africa, but with Mark Taylor established as the leading outside-centre, I was someone who was filling in for others, whether it be at inside-centre, outside-centre or on the wing. I saw myself very much as an outside-centre, but Mark's style was more suited to the game Henry wanted to play and, at the age of 34, I was just glad to be involved. Having refused to return to Wales to play, it would have been no surprise had Henry shown me the door. I was getting on and outside-centre was probably the most hotly contested position in the Wales squad. Henry was a coach who placed a significant emphasis on form and the fact that I had always been someone who enjoyed training and who made sure that I was always physically sharp kept me in the set-up at a time when other coaches may just have wished me all the best.

I nearly did not make it for the World Cup. The calf injury I had picked up in Paris flared up again when we were training in Brecon and when we went to Portugal for our final week's preparations, I could not take part in any of the sessions and spent the week sunbathing. I feared that I would be dropped from the squad, but I was named even though I could not take part in the opening match against Argentina. The eyes of the rugby world were on Wales that day and, in time-honoured fashion, it rained. The match was not memorable, but we held on for victory. Scott Gibbs had been hit by food poisoning in the days leading up to the game and he had to be replaced in the second half by Jason Jones-Hughes. This was the Welsh public's first real chance to see what all the fuss had been about. He did well enough, but his next outing was on the wing and it proved that centre was without question his best position.

Our second match was against Japan and I played on the wing. I scored a try early on, but after 30 minutes my calf went again and I had to come off. I would not have been surprised if Henry had replaced me in the squad, but he kept me on and, after missing the defeat against Samoa, I was on the bench for the quarter-final against Australia. Failing to beat the Samoans meant that we had to wait for the last match of our group, Argentina against Japan, before knowing whether we would finish top of our pool. If Japan had won, we would have been off to Murrayfield to face Scotland in the quarter-final play-offs because Samoa would have finished top by virtue of their victory over us. If Argentina won, it would leave three teams level at the top and it would then come down to points difference. To finish top, the Pumas had to score some 70 points, but they seemed motivated by the fact that if they won and finished third in the group, they would make the play-offs and face Ireland in Lille rather than Scotland in Edinburgh. They achieved their target and duly beat the Irish to make the last eight for the first time and we ended up topping the group and preparing for the visit of the World Cup favourites, Australia.

They had only conceded one try in their pool matches in Ireland and it was their defence which was ultimately to take them to the title. We pushed them all the way, but it was uphill after the Wallabies were awarded an early try which we felt should have been disallowed for an accidental off-side. The New Zealand referee Colin Hawke was booed off the pitch at the end after Australia had been awarded a try despite a knock-on in the build-up. Perhaps he did not have the greatest of games, but the result was a fair one even if the scoreboard did not tell the true story of how close it had been. I feel that it is often the case that referees, probably subconsciously, award 50–50 decisions to the side which is expected to win. It had been 10–9 to Australia at half-time and Neil Jenkins just missed a drop goal in the third quarter which would have given us the lead. Ben Tune scored a crucial try with 16 minutes to go and George Gregan rubbed it in after Tim Horan had dropped the ball. I came on for the final 28 minutes, replacing Gareth Thomas on the wing, and I thoroughly enjoyed the experience. It had not been that long ago that pundits were saying Wales were not worthy of hosting the World Cup because we were a laughing stock on the field. We showed that we had improved considerably and we gave Australia a harder game than France were to manage in the final at the Millennium Stadium.

The end was an anti-climax, even if we had not been expected to defeat Australia. We had to check out of our hotel the following day and some players became emotional. For many, it was an experience they would not savour again but to me it was something that had to be accepted. You had to look forward, move on and get out. I had assumed that it would be my only World Cup campaign and it was hard for me because I was never fully fit. I was always battling to be ready for the next game and in all I tasted less than an hour of action. The tournament showed that defence wins matches and it was only South Africa who came near to Australia in that regard.

Graham Henry changed the way we played after that to take what Australia had taught us on board, but it did not meet with success initially and when England beat us 44–15 at the Millennium Stadium in 2001, he took some of their game on board, in particular the need to get back-row forwards working out wide. When we had beaten Japan, it marked our 10th consecutive victory, a remarkable run considering where we had come from. The game against Samoa should have been our 11th, but we failed to nail them down and allowed them to counter-attack their way to victory. It was never quite the same after the World Cup as mental fatigue caught up with the players. We had played 16 internationals under Henry in 14 months, on top of our club demands, and as we were operating with a smaller pool of players than most countries, it took its toll. The subsequent Six Nations campaign was a disappointment and we have still to move up to the level where we can compete with the best on an equal footing.

My experience in English rugby had convinced me that in terms of raw talent, Wales were as good as England but they struggled when it came to organisation. There was a depth to the English league which meant that virtually every game was competitive: there were no free lunches. In Wales, Cardiff and Swansea had pulled out of the league and the Heineken Cup the season before the World Cup in protest at what they felt was the uncompetitive nature of the game there, with too many walkovers and not enough meaningful matches. The Welsh Rugby Union saw salvation in a British – or an Anglo-Welsh – league, an admission that they were not in charge of their own destiny.

The 1999 World Cup proved a failure for all four home unions. Ireland failed to reach the quarter-finals and Wales, England and Scotland watched the semi-finals on television. The three major southern hemisphere countries had all made the last four, proof again that the partnership they forged below international level in the Super 12 series meant that they grew stronger together. In Europe, all we had was the Heineken Cup, a competition in which not all the top players appear and which was used as a political football. Was it any wonder that none of our countries had ever won the World Cup? As the banners and bunting were taken down in Cardiff after the 1999 final, the talk was of lessons being learned, which meant the home unions working together. Wales and Scotland pushed for a British league and the club owners in England were tilting towards an agreement when the Rugby Football Union persuaded them of the merits of a one-nation policy and the chance was lost.

England picked up after the 1999 World Cup and in the 2001 championship they looked the best side in the world having already defeated South Africa and Australia at Twickenham. They defeated us by a record margin in Cardiff with some ruthless finishing. The statistics after the match showed that we had not missed many tackles, but statistics lie. Mark Taylor and I tend to go out of our way to make a tackle where others sometimes hold back. Taylor and I try to fill holes and if we end up failing to nail someone, it goes down as a missed tackle – but if we did not attempt to cover the ground, it would not show up in the statistics. England scored some of their tries because our players were not running wide to make tackles, staying in their own channels. The stats showed that we had most of the ball and applied most of the pressure, but England scored the points. The previous week, Cardiff and Swansea had been well beaten in the Heineken Cup quarter-final at Gloucester and Leicester respectively and, apart from the Grannygate affair, it was the only time I had seen Graham Henry lose his composure. He had been chosen to coach the Lions in Australia in the summer of 2001 and it was clear that the bulk of the squad were going to be English. It was small wonder that we took some of England's tactics on board for the rest of that championship, just as we had after Australia in the World Cup, but the time had to come when we would lead, not follow.

THIRTEEN

LUCKY NUMBER

_____

If I was starting my career now, it is highly unlikely that I would play in the centre. I would be regarded as too small, which was the case even back in 1984 when Maesteg wanted me to spend a season away from them, getting fattened up at junior level. They tried to convince me that my future lay on the wing and it was a time back then when rugby union was developing an obsession with the crash ball, using a big centre to batter his way through the middle and set up second-phase possession. There always has to be room for artistry and the fact that someone like Jonathan Davies, a mercurial outside-half, could succeed in the hard-bitten world of rugby league proved that sport is about balance and choosing players who complement each other.

The best centre combination I have seen in rugby union was Jeremy Guscott and Scott Gibbs on the Lions tour of South Africa in 1997. Gibbs played down a narrow channel. His game was not multi-dimensional, but he was ruthless and clinical, uncompromising in defence and attack. He was the player around whom the others grouped in that series. A quiet man off the field, it was Scott who did the urging and the shouting rather than the captain, Martin Johnson. It was a shock when he was left out of the squad for Australia in 2001. He had not been at his best for a couple of years and Graham Henry's gameplan of setting up sequences with the ball released at the point of contact did not suit his style. Henry's contention was that the more phases you kept the ball for, the more disrupted the opposition would become, but this policy was flawed, as England demonstrated by keeping their shape in Cardiff in February 2001. Seven was Henry's magic number in terms of phases, but strong defences will not allow you to get anywhere near that number. Scott's strength lay in committing tacklers and setting up the ball, but Henry wanted the ball to be transferred quickly. I still thought the Lions would have taken advantage of the presence Scott brings to a dressing-room or a training session. The bigger the occasion, the better he performs and it was a brave call to leave him behind.

Even though Scott and I played for Neath in 1990 and resumed our partnership with Wales seven years later, it was only in the 2000–01 season that I started to get to know him. Like me, he does not have much time for rugby small talk and he values his private life. He and I are totally different players and we are not similar characters. His response to being left out of the Australia tour was to make himself unavailable for Wales's tour to Japan that summer on the grounds that he did not want to accept second best. Unlike him, I had not been surprised at being overlooked for Australia and so my disappointment was not as deep, but I did not see Japan as a consolation. You should not pick and choose when it comes to international rugby because it is an honour to play for your country. Tens of thousands of players take up the game with the dream of representing their nation, but only an élite few manage it and I would never turn down Wales. Scott had his reasons and I respect them. Like me, he is not one to say something that he does not mean and it was better for him to pull out of Japan than go there letting everyone know that he would rather be elsewhere.

He will go down, rightly, as one of Welsh rugby's greats, a player who proved himself with the Lions in 1993 as well as 1997. His try at Wembley in 1999 in the final minute against England will never be forgotten and I enjoyed playing alongside him. He committed defenders and that provided the space I thrived on. We were more effective as a pair under Kevin Bowring than Graham Henry because we played a deeper, wider game under Bowring. There was a footballing side to Scott that few coaches chose to exploit. He was far more than a crash-baller, but as union became obsessed with size and strength, so his 15st frame was exploited more than his hands. There were suggestions after he had been left out of the Australia tour that his international career was at an end, but at the age of 30 he still had a lot more to offer.

Jeremy Guscott, like me, was an outside-centre. For years, he represented the only footballing instinct in an efficient, powerful but boring England side. The Lions chose not to play to his strengths in 1997, a decision which was vindicated by the fact that they won the series, but he was a player who always had to be watched because he could change a game in an instant. Whereas Scott was straight and uncompromising, there was a touch of arrogance about Jerry, which made it hard for some to get on with him off the field. He knew he was good and was not going to pretend otherwise. If I were picking a rugby union team made up of the best players I have appeared with or against, he would wear the number 13 jersey ahead of the likes of Joe Stanley, Frank Bunce, Jason Little or Robbie Fleck. He was the best outside-centre in the world in his time, and the pity was that he was not part of a team that wanted to exploit his talents fully. How he would revel in the new England.

If I were picking a rugby team made up of the best players I have encountered in league and union though, the centres would be the Australians Laurie Daley and Andrew Ettingshausen. Daley had hands and vision to die for while Ettingshausen was the best defender I have come across. Between them, they had everything and they would have succeeded at the highest levels in rugby union. Gary Connolly was the best British centre I played against – behind the two Australians but a footballer of rare quality who made things happen. Another Australian, Steve Renouf, who went on to play for Wigan, was the opponent I found it hardest to play against. He once stood me up and went outside me as if I were not there. I pride myself on my defence, but he destroyed me and he made me look at my game.

Another reason why I think I would struggle to establish myself in the centre is that my kicking and handling skills are not good enough. I can virtually remember every occasion I have kicked the ball out of hand, which says everything and Maesteg immediately identified handling as a weakness in my game. Playing rugby league in Australia showed me how I was lacking in variety. Australian players had all the skills; they were multi-dimensional footballers who had a hard competitive edge to go with their natural ability, and probably the most satisfying time of my career was when I showed I could hold my own playing rugby league Down Under. You would take three or four days to recover from games because they were so physically and mentally draining. Playing union has never affected me in such a way. Even at the age of 36, I feel pretty good the morning after a match.

The Ireland centre Brian O'Driscoll is a player whose career I will be watching with interest. He has balance, good hands and his defence is excellent. He is sharp off the mark, brave and he makes things happen. He is virtually Scott Gibbs and me rolled into one. He needs regular exposure in big matches. Outside of the Heineken Cup and playing international rugby, he has had little in the way of meaningful rugby. The Celtic league, which Scotland, Ireland and Wales arranged from the start of the 2001–02 season was timely for him, but if Celtic players like O'Driscoll are to fulfil their full potential, they either have to join an English club or hope that the four home unions come up with a domestic programme which is based on the southern hemisphere principle of growing strong together.

There have been some in England whose response to one-sided Six Nations campaigns was to call for England and France to pull out of the tournament and join up with Australia, New Zealand and South Africa. That would be an act of folly because it would shrink the game at the top. Playing in the rugby league World Cup in 1995 was an enjoyable experience for me, but you knew who was going to win the tournament before a ball was kicked. Ireland and Scotland have started to field teams, but they are stuffed full of Australians who have discovered long-lost grandparents. It was a small World Cup and union should be looking to expand. Playing a super Five Nations Championship every year would devalue the World Cup and probably lead to its ruin. The top five countries would cream off the money in the sport, development programmes in other parts of the world would end and where would the players of tomorrow come from? The former England captain Will Carling was right when he called, at the end of the 2000–01 season, for the leading club competitions in Britain and Ireland to be scrapped and a two-division

European super league, made up of teams from the four home unions and France and Italy, to be set up. The emphasis has to be on expansion. Italy have not brought much yet to the Six Nations, but better to involve them and help their game improve than to fob them off with a few meaningless friendlies.

Administrators are only too quick to point out if players don't have much in the way of vision on the field, but they have to look at themselves. Where is British rugby going? Too many clubs are in hock to their owners, one bounced cheque away from ruin. There is no long-term planning and the game is living beyond its means with salaries unrealistic. The top players in England earn more than their Welsh counterparts, but otherwise wage levels are roughly the same. After the collapse of Richmond and London Scottish, players became more aware politically, and in 2001 there was an alliance between the top clubs and the players, a partnership some Welsh sides were later to enter into. We were fortunate at Richmond to all find other clubs. All we lost financially was 20 per cent of our wages for four months. When I joined Northampton, my contract started at the point my deal with Richmond ended so I was never out of work, but the position for many of us could have been serious and it is right that the players are effectively part of a trade union because livelihoods are at stake.

Even though my career has straddled three decades, there have been few opponents who I lost respect for. Other players come from the field with tales of dastardly deeds which were perpetrated against them, such as kicking, gouging, spitting and sledging, but no one has ever tried to put the frighteners on me. When Wales played South Africa in November 2000, their centre, Robbie Fleck, had a lot to say for himself, bad-mouthing everyone except me, his opposite number. Perhaps he did not think I was worth it, but he behaved like a complete prat and in the old days he would not have lasted the 80 minutes. He niggled all the time, calling players names and handing out sly kicks and punches. Perhaps he felt he had something to lose, but when I read that he had blown a match in the 2001 Super 12 series by dawdling to the posts after making a scything break and having the ball knocked out of his grasp at the moment he was about to touch down for a try, it made me smile. Fleck is a world-class centre but he needs to grow up.

In rugby league, Manly Sea Eagles winger John Hopoate was the most unpleasant character I came across. My last game for Cronulla was against Manly and our full-back had an 80 minutes that he would not be submitting on any future CV. He dropped virtually every high ball that came his way and two of his misses led to tries. Nothing was going right for him, but no one tries to have a bad game; they just happen sometimes. Hopoate was in his face all the time, telling him how useless he was and it said everything about Hopoate. He was banned for three months in 2001 for an offence committed on the field so disgusting it is not worth going into detail about it here. He did it three times in one match, and it was only when it was reported that other players who had also suffered at his hands came forward. He was lucky to just get three months. There should be no place in the game for players like that.

I was delighted for Will Greenwood when he re-emerged as an international player in the 2001 Six Nations. He would not have been out of place in the Lions' Test team in 1997, but after that tour, he struggled to fulfil his potential and ended up moving from Leicester back to Harlequins. I like the way he is able to off-load the ball no matter how much pressure he finds himself under. A centre comfortable playing inside or outside, he is to me more dangerous as an outside-centre because he has the eye for a gap and the pace and strength to get through it. He scored three tries against Wales at the Millennium Stadium and was nearly in for a fourth before I tackled him. I had come on to the pitch for the last 20 minutes because Mark Taylor's lack of match practice had caught up with him.

I have never been comfortable with the substitute's role. It takes you at least 15 minutes to find your feet by which time, in most instances, the final whistle has gone. My only other appearance in the 2001 championship was as a temporary replacement against Italy in Rome when Taylor had to go off for stitches after a nasty cut on his head. I did not expect him to come back on, but he did and I was restricted to a seven-minute walk-on role. I was not sure whether it constituted a cap, until someone pointed out that I could have scored a try and you could hardly have an uncapped player among the scorers. Graham Henry does not like handing out caps for the sake of it and does not bring on players for sentimental reasons, which is fair enough. Equally, there are times when you would like to know why you have not been brought on, as was the case with me in Paris in 2001. I had stayed on the bench for the previous match against Scotland in Murrayfield even though Taylor had again showed signs of slowing down – hardly surprising after his long lay-off following a knee operation. He ended up missing a tackle he would normally have made in his sleep.

Scott Gibbs was brought off against France after 50 minutes. He had not had his best match in a Wales jersey, but he had just helped set up a try. When he knew that his number was up, Scott presumed that I would be replacing him. Instead Henry sent on Stephen Jones, who had played at outside-half and full-back for Wales. Henry saw Stephen as the eventual inside-centre replacement for Scott, but it was a big call to make in an important match and, even allowing for Henry's reluctance to explain why he had made a decision, he said nothing to me or to Scott. I should have gone up to him and asked, and it did beg the questions of what I was doing on the bench and who I was covering for. The wings, Gareth Thomas and Dafydd James, were both outside-centres by preference and I assumed that I was covering Taylor and the wing, but I had thought that I would also be the replacement at inside-centre.

I had asked Henry the previous year why I was still in the squad. I had assumed that after the World Cup I would be sent back to Northampton to see out my career on the basis that I was not likely to be around in 2003. Henry was still adopting a flat backline and there was not enough freedom in that to suit my style. His reply was that I was there to do a job for him, but he did not elaborate. I was not complaining because I wanted to remain in the squad, but not just for the sake of it. One disadvantage of playing in Northampton was that I was never up against my rivals (Mark Taylor, Dafydd James, Jamie Robinson, Leigh Davies, Jason Jones-Hughes and Gareth Thomas) for a place in the Wales side. I suspect that Henry liked my attitude in training, and I was surprised when I was asked whether I would be available to tour Japan in the summer of 2001 because I thought he would take the opportunity to look at younger players. He did in the sense that 18-year-old Cardiff flanker Robin Sowden-Taylor was chosen even though he had never started a first-class match. He was half my age, young enough to be my son (and his Christian name gave the other players an excuse to go on about Batman and Robin). In my last year at Northampton, they had a young centre, Chris Hyndman, who shared the same birthday as me. Come March that year, he turned 18 just as I was denying claims that I was 36. Age is all in the mind though. Frank Bunce was playing in the centre for New Zealand when he was 37 and I do not believe in approaching a season thinking you will call it a day because of how old you are. You know it will be time to pack it in when your performances are no longer good enough and your rivals are disappearing over the horizon. There is no way that I will play on just for the sake of it. When the finger beckons, I will not hang around.

At the start of the 2000–01 international season, the players set themselves the goal of winning six of the eight matches Wales were scheduled to play, as well as the Triple Crown – something Wales had not achieved since 1988. I am all for setting targets, but you have to be realistic and also give yourself every chance of attaining them. The problem with our stating the Triple Crown as an aim was that our first championship match was England. If we lost that we'd have no chance of succeeding. Far better to have set out to finish no lower than second in the Six Nations because one defeat would not have made the objective unattainable. Some players had set the target of winning every match, but again, one defeat and you have failed. Henry left it up to the players to draw up the aims for the season, and in the event the 'six out of eight' target was not unrealistic.

We had lost to South Africa in the November having been in charge at one point. Henry was criticised for bringing off Neil Jenkins with 20 minutes to go and replacing him with Arwel Thomas. Arwel is a rare player in the modern game, someone who likes to do things off the cuff and he often confuses his team-mates more than the opposition. At the top level, you have to be organised and know what you are doing, which is why Neil is as good an outside-half as I have ever come across. He bosses a game, and while he may not have Arwel's capacity to make a break out of nowhere, he is every bit as creative. That said, there was nothing wrong with Henry giving Arwel a go against the Springboks. We had just fallen behind, having dominated the match in terms of possession, and Arwel had shown for Swansea that season an ability to keep the scoreboard moving by dropping goals from everywhere. It did not work against South Africa, and Neil was to finish the season dropping goals for fun, but the whole point of having players on the bench is to use them tactically and not just wait for someone to get injured. Arwel was unfortunate in that twice when he was lining up drop goals, players inadvertently got in his way. It was a brave attempt to win the game and much of the subsequent criticism was more to do with the fact that a number of pundits had been waiting to have a go at Henry rather than because they strongly disagreed with the substitution.

England did me a favour because Henry changed his gameplan after the defeat. He took some stick in the media because we had looked wooden and shapeless in comparison and the pressure got to him. Even though we turned a certain victory into a draw against Scotland the following match, it had been a marked improvement on what had gone before and we followed it up with our second consecutive victory in Paris – the first time a Wales team had achieved that since the 1950s. We ended the season by beating Italy in Rome which gave us four wins and a draw out of seven. The international against Ireland at the Millennium Stadium had to be put forward to the following October because of the foot-and-mouth outbreak in Britain.

If I had not been a centre, I would probably not have played rugby. Standing out on the wing held no appeal to me and I did not have the range of skills needed to play in either of the half-back positions. There was no way I would have chanced my arm in the forwards: you have to be a head-case to put yourself through some of the things those guys have to endure. They wear the scars of battle, and while I have every admiration for them, especially the front-rowers who inhabit a world of their own, all the money in the game would not persuade me to join their number.

I have never been superstitious about wearing the number 13 jersey – far from it. I tended to be numbered at 12 with Neath because Colin Laity and then Scott Gibbs played at 13. Some players will not wear 13 under any circumstances, but in my second spell with Wales both Leigh Davies and Mark Taylor wanted the jersey. I tended to get my own way with Leigh, but Mark and I agreed that whoever was down at 13 in the programme would be given the number. I had to play at 12 a couple of times before I got hold of John Rowlands, the chief assistant with the squad, and told him to make sure that I was put at number 13 in the programme and it worked a treat. I regard 13 as a lucky number, but more than that it is the traditional number for an outside-centre. Call me contrary, but it is better to be the exception than the rule!

The centre position may have changed in the years I have been playing, but the longer I have been around the more I have come to appreciate that sport operates in a circle – what goes around comes around. Jonah Lomu set a new trend for wings when he became the player of the 1995 World Cup, trampling everything and everyone in his path. He was like a runaway tank, a devastating combination of speed and power and suddenly everyone wanted to discover the next Jonah Lomu. Big became beautiful as far as wings went and a number of centres found themselves converted to the flanks. The balance was redressed in the following World Cup when Christophe Dominici and Philippe Bernat-Salles led the All Blacks a merry dance at Twickenham in the semi-final.

Shane Williams had an impressive championship for Wales in 2000, but was then left out the following year. Shane is the opposite of Lomu, a diminutive wing who is at his best when given the chance to go around opponents. To play him, you need to give him space and the game Wales favoured at the start of the 2001 Six Nations was geared to strength more than speed, but his day will come. No matter how much fitter and stronger players become, there is no substitute for speed and there never will be.

FOURTEEN

MARCHING IN

I started my career in Wales at a club whose name held religious connotations (Maesteg was known as 'the Old Parish'), and I finished my English leg of it at Northampton, a club called 'the Saints' long before rugby union hijacked an idea from rugby league and sloganised clubs in a bid to give them a new popularity (Leeds Tykes and Sale Sharks, for example; at least Cronulla Sharks went the distance and called their ground Shark Park). I had two happy years at Northampton, though I felt slightly sinned against when it came to the end. I would have seen out my career there but I was given a 'maybe' when I had asked for a yes or a no and Neath moved in.

Northampton had made a move for me during my final year in London, and I hoped they would come back in for me when the Richmond club was sacrificed by English First Division Rugby Ltd. Part of the attraction was the chance to work again with Ian McGeechan who rang me up after Bristol had made me an attractive offer. I met Geech at a service station on the M1 and said yes there and then, but by the time I started training with the club, at the end of the 1999 World Cup, he had taken up a new job in charge of the Scotland side. Geech had wanted to stay at Northampton for the final year of his contract, effectively doing two jobs part-time, but the Saints' owner Keith Barwell refused to consider the idea and John Steele, whom I knew from his days with Richmond's tenants at the Athletic Ground, London Scottish, was appointed in his place. The

Welsh squad teased me that Geech had gone because he could not face working with me again. Geech was a factor in my joining Northampton and I was very sorry to see him go, but I would have signed for the club anyway.

Another reason I wanted to join Northampton was to do with the crowd at Franklin's Gardens. When I played there for Richmond, it more than any other club, reminded me of Neath – far more so than the likes of Gloucester, Leicester and Bath. It was not just the noise generated but the fact that attendances were high no matter who the opposition was. In my last season there, we played Rotherham, the bottom club. The match was televised live but a crowd of more than 9,000 still turned up. Northampton was a rugby town and in that sense it was more Welsh than English. Bristol had sold their ground to Bristol Rovers and, though I would have been as well-off there financially as I would have been at Northampton, and far closer to Wales, there was no choice to make in the end.

Keith Barwell was a totally different owner to Ashley Levett. For a start, he had an emotional, as well as financial, investment in the club having followed Northampton all his life. He was astute and did not throw his money away. I negotiated a set wage and any bonuses were at Barwell's discretion. It was different to rugby league, and Richmond initially, but it was the way I preferred. We were told that winning a cup or finishing in the top four of the league could lead to a bonus, but it did not dominate your thinking, as it did the players at Warrington. When we won the Heineken Cup in 2000, we each received £12,000, a welcome sum in what had been the most physically and emotionally draining season of my career. Other clubs, like Cardiff, offer bonuses more indiscriminately; their players get an extra 10 per cent of their wages for making the Heineken Cup quarter-finals, another 10 per cent if they make the semis and a further 10 per cent for winning the trophy. The club has not had to pay out much yet. Bonuses should be for achievement, not for making up the numbers.

Success is incentive enough for players. I accepted Northampton's offer without haggling. It was the same in 2001 when I joined Neath. I had been offered a better contract by Bristol, but Neath had some of my wages defrayed by the Welsh Rugby Union because I was a squad player and it felt right to be returning to the club that had kick-started my international career. I knew the Neath coach Lyn Jones well, which helped, and when I joined Northampton, I was linking up again with Nick Beal, Paul Grayson, Tim Rodber and Matt Dawson who had all been on the Lions tour to South Africa in 1997. It is always easier to fit into a new club when you know people.

I think Geech regretted not seeing his final year out at Northampton, and not just because we won the Heineken Cup. Had he stayed, I am sure that he would have made himself available to coach the Lions in Australia in 2001. The Lions made every effort to persuade him to take charge for the fourth consecutive tour, but Geech felt he had to commit himself to Scotland. I met him not long before the Lions left for Perth and you could tell that he was unsure whether or not he had made the right decision. He embodies all that the Lions stand for, and I would not be surprised if he put himself in the frame for the 2005 visit to New Zealand, the only one of the three Lions touring countries where he has not enjoyed a series victory either as a player or as a coach.

I never experienced a Geech training session with Northampton. By the time I started with the club after Wales had been knocked out of the World Cup, he had gone. John Steele was seen as an obvious successor. He had played for Northampton for ten years and he had built up a reputation as a coach who was strong on organisation, befitting a former army officer. He was a calm, approachable man but he did not really add anything to our game after Geech had left. In the 2000 close season, he tried to impose himself by making our style more expansive. We had been a club which had set a premium on establishing a dominance at forward, but we lost three of our first four matches and Steele quickly reverted to McGeechan's methods. He had wanted the ball to go through the outside-centre and full-back channels, which suited me, but we struggled when we ran out of forwards out wide and the experiment did not last long.

My role was to organise the defence and I was comfortable with that. I have always seen myself as a centre whose strengths are better suited to defence than attack. I picked up the nickname 'The Clamp' during my rugby league days, something I was not keen on, but defence *is* essential in the modern game. You sometimes hear people saying: 'They looked good every time the opposition had the ball', and one of the reasons Australia won the 1999 World Cup was that they exerted tremendous pressure in defence. Even when England adopted a running game after that, their defence was still strong and it is the foundation that underpins every successful side. Leicester carried everything before them in the 2000–01 season and there was no defence more difficult to break down in England. Even Stade Français found it impossible in the Heineken Cup final.

Northampton had a strong squad when I joined them and I knew they were ready to challenge for trophies whereas Bristol and Newport, who had also made me offers, were in the rebuilding process. As well as their Lions, Northampton boasted the likes of Jon Sleightholme, Pat Lam, Federico Mendez, Budge Pountney and Gary Pagel. I knew Andy Northey from my days with Warrington: he was once sent off for a high tackle on me. He became a rival of mine in the centre, but we developed a strong friendship and it was the same in Wales with the likes of Leigh Davies, Mark Taylor and Gareth Thomas. Some players like to blank their rivals and say nothing more than hello to them, but I am not into back-biting or back-stabbing. May the best man get the jersey, I say, and I have never been one to pretend that there are no deficiencies in my game. I am as competitive as anyone, but rivalries remain on the field.

My first match for Northampton was at home to Gloucester. We lost, but after that we gathered momentum and within a few months we were challenging for trophies on three fronts: the league, the Tetley's Bitter Cup and – the biggest prize of them all – the Heineken Cup. We started to splutter only when the Six Nations started up and we lost a number of players to the various squads. We started to slide down the league, but we made the final of the Tetley's Bitter Cup and we knew that victory over Wasps would secure our place in the Heineken Cup the following season. There were three routes into European club rugby's main tournament: finishing in the top five of the league, winning the domestic cup or being crowned Heineken Cup champions. Playing in the Heineken Cup is financially lucrative, and we found ourselves before the end of that season in the anomalous position of concentrating as hard on making sure we were involved the following October (2000) as we were on the latter stages of that year's competition.

The group stage of the Heineken Cup meant a return to my old stamping ground, Neath, but the only survivor from my playing days was the back-rower Rowland Phillips, who had returned to the Gnoll after spending most of the 1990s in rugby league. One of the strange aspects of my career is that though I have been with six different clubs, the only time I played against my former team-mates was after I had left Maesteg for Neath. The Gnoll was not quite as packed as I had remembered it from my days there. Neath were only in the Heineken Cup because Cardiff and Swansea had pulled out and they had suffered during the summer after nearly going broke. Lyn had lost a number of his players after contracts had been broken because of a lack of means to honour them, and their priority was to get through the season. We doubled Neath and Edinburgh, but struggled in both our matches against Grenoble. We finished at the top of our group and were drawn at home to Wasps in the quarter-final.

I only lasted 20 minutes against Wasps before going off with a rib injury. We needed the crowd behind us that day because, in all truth, we were outplayed. Paul Grayson's boot kept us in the match and he was enjoying a vintage season with his goal-kicking. Without him, we would not have made the Heineken Cup final; for a player who had battled as hard against injury as Paul, it was a fitting way for his career to finish. Wasps thought they had us, but Paul was going through a period when he did not miss anything and every indiscretion was ruthlessly punished. We were in the semi-finals where Llanelli and Scott Quinnell awaited us at Richmond's former home, the Madejski Stadium. Whatever happened, I knew it was going to be a bittersweet day for me because I knew all the Llanelli players and I wanted a Welsh team to win the Heineken Cup – but not in 2000.

I spoke to Scott the week before the game and we wished each other all the best. I am not sure that he meant it though because he smashed me with two late tackles during the game. As we got off the coach at the ground, I was accosted by a large group of Llanelli supporters who shouted 'traitor' at me, good naturedly. I gave them some back: 'All this just for me? Thanks.' It was that sort of day: a near-capacity crowd basking in warm May sunshine. The Welsh contingent had placards bearing the words 'Ben Who?', a reference to a comment made by the Northampton and England wing Ben Cohen after England's victory over Wales at Twickenham that May. When asked how he had thought the Wales wing Shane Williams had played, Ben replied 'Shane Who?' It was meant to be an off-the-cuff remark as England gloried in their victory, but it backfired and Ben was portrayed as arrogant and lacking grace. He would have been better off mouthing a platitude, but he was a young man in a hurry and did not stop to think. A few months later he received death threats from Wales fans along the lines of 'We will kill you' and 'We will blow you up'. The police were called in and it did unsettle Ben who rewarded the Llanelli crowd by making a couple of unforced errors early in the game, but the banter was good humoured and he recovered to score a try.

I claimed an early try after we had put pressure on the Llanelli line. I thought the ball should have come out earlier, but the forwards rumbled on. Eventually, Nick Beal received a pass and had the strength to hold a couple of tacklers before flicking the ball over the top. All I had to do was catch it to score and I felt so embarrassed that I could not celebrate. I did not want to be seen to be revelling in the disappointment of friends, but actually the job was far from done. Llanelli hit back at us in the second half and, as the rigours of a hard season caught up with us, they looked the stronger side in the final quarter. Pat Lam had to go off with an injury and we were running on our reserve tank. Had Llanelli played their traditionally expansive game, I am sure they would have won, but they kept it tight and launched a series of close-range drives which were repulsed without much difficulty.

The match looked as if it would go into extra-time, which would not have suited us, when Ian Boobyer gave away a needless penalty at a ruck. Everyone was anxious at that stage and the moment would haunt Boobs for months to come. Paul Grayson was presented with a 45-yard kick at goal to the right of the posts, but the form he was in it may as well have been smack in front of them. Over it went and we were through to the final at Twickenham where we would meet the Irish champions Munster. I did not spend much time celebrating on the pitch; I had a couple of drinks with Scott afterwards. Llanelli were shattered having got so close to the final and I felt uneasy about beating them, until a few days later when I heard their coach, Gareth

Jenkins, say that he would rather any team other than Northampton won the final. It was a comment which did not become him. Llanelli only had themselves to blame: only they knew why they kept it tight when their threat lay out wide.

That summer, Scott spent a couple of days at my house near Northampton and I made him watch a video of the match on a cinema-size screen. The replay did not look any better to him than the actual match. We were out for a walk in Northampton when a woman came rushing up to me.

'Is Scott Quinnell going to be signing for Northampton?' she asked.

'I do not like starting rumours,' I replied. She walked off, only to return immediately.

'Who are you, anyway?'

I saw her at Franklin's Gardens later in the season and she apologised: her husband had sent her to talk to me and had only afterwards let her know who I was. It made Scott feel a little better.

Pat Lam had finished the semi-final exhorting us on from the touch-line, much to Llanelli's disgust. He personified the essence of Northampton: he believed in team spirit and, a religious man, he would get us to bow our heads and pray before matches. He regarded the squad as a family and the social aspect of the game was very important to him. He would divide us into sub-committees, looking after aspects like videos on the bus for away matches, events and functions. I had seen during the World Cup just how players followed him. He had led Samoa to victory at the Millennium Stadium, crowning his afternoon with an 80-yard try. Pat has real charisma and he is one of the best players around. I could not believe it when I heard that Northampton were letting him go at the end of the 2000–01 season. He had missed some matches because of a shoulder injury, but I had presumed that when his playing days ended he would have ended up on the coaching staff. The only reason given for his departure was the £1.8 million salary cap and that young back-rowers were coming through at the club (which was true as far as it went) but only a couple of days later I was offered a new one-year deal. I was three years older than Pat and there were as many young centres at the club as there were back-row forwards.

Perhaps John Steele saw him as a threat. He did not give that impression, but I heard from others afterwards that he did. Pat called a press conference to announce that he was going, which did not please John or the club. It caused a lot of hassle and Pat later apologised. I could see his reasoning: better to get journalists together to tell them why, rather than have them ring him all through the week. As a family man, Pat values his privacy at home. The reason for his action, though, was that he, like the rest of us, did not properly understand the decision. His playing days were coming to an end, but he still had something to offer. It was no surprise then, when he accepted a one-year contract to return to Newcastle. Pat knew Graham Henry well from their days with Auckland and was sounded out for the job of Wales forwards' coach. He turned it down because he wanted to carry on playing for another season, but I would not be surprised if the offer is repeated when he does retire. He may not have had much experience of coaching, but in terms of motivation and knowledge, he is up there with the best, and we became close friends during our time at Northampton.

After Llanelli came the Tetley's Bitter Cup final. It was another Twickenham let-down for me: I had never won at the ground and Wasps were too good for us. They played all the rugby and, again, it was only Paul Grayson's boot which kept us in touch. We looked a tired side, in danger of challenging for everything and winning nothing. The league had long gone and Wasps kept the door shut on us until the end when Craig Moir was bundled into touch just short of the line. Everyone had been going on about how fatigue was getting to us and we did not need much persuading that this was the case. We had lost five matches in a row in the league and we needed to win at Newcastle in the last match of the season before Munster to finish in the top five and confirm our place in the following season's Heineken Cup. We had to dig deep, but we got there.

It meant we could relax against Munster. The atmosphere at Twickenham was more electric than I had experienced during an international. The Munster supporters were outstanding and, as usual, ours turned out in force. Keith Barwell had laid on free buses for them from Northampton and a couple of dozen coaches motored down the M1 for the game. We spent the Friday night in the same hotel in Weybridge that the 1997 Lions had gathered in before leaving for South Africa. We treated it as a normal away match, except Pat's prayers took slightly longer. It was another warm day and the match was as close as we had expected.

Munster scored the only try of the afternoon, but Paul's boot gave us a 9–8 victory. We had struggled to build anything in terms of attacking momentum and once again our forwards led the way. Ronan O'Gara had two chances at the end to win the match with long-range penalties, but he pulled both of them wide. We had had a similar let-off in the Tetley's Bitter Cup semi-final against Saracens when a dropped goal looked to have gone over. A New Zealand referee was in charge that day and Pat shouted at him that the ball had gone wide and not to give the score. The official's hand stayed down and we celebrated – but not as wildly as when the final whistle went against Munster. Their supporters applauded us despite their disappointment and it was, without any doubt, the highlight of my club career.

Pat collected the trophy and quickly went on to the pitch to parade it to the supporters. Security officials at Twickenham were mortified because they had not had time to grab hold of the cup and replace it with a replica trophy, as was the custom. The real thing only ever makes a fleeting appearance before being locked back up in a bank vault. Pat was not to know though, and as we did our lap of honour, the security men were puffing and wheezing their way around the pitch, melting in the heat, trying to get their hands on the trophy. They had to wait until we returned to the dressing-room where they closely examined it before finding, to their immense relief, that it had not been damaged in any way.

I had gone into the dressing-room as the celebrations were raging on the field because I was shattered. Budge Pountney was there and we found a huge bottle of champagne. While the other players were still parading the genuine Heineken Cup we thought we would get in there first. Off came the cork, but to our great disappointment the contents were vintage Heineken. We were celebrating one of the best days of our careers. Twickenham put on a finger buffet before we returned to Franklin's Gardens which was packed with thousands of supporters. The players stood at the bottom of the pitch, with the replica cup, and walked up in line.

I had a couple of beers but suddenly found that all the players had gone. A nightclub in the town had opened up for them and they had all gone without telling me. I walked there with some supporters and it started to rain. I was drenched by the time I arrived and Nicola, who was already there, was wondering where I had been. We had a room downstairs to ourselves and Nicola put her credit card behind the bar to save us having to find change all the time. Keith Barwell went upstairs, where it was packed, congratulated the Saints on a memorable victory and said that all the drinks were on him for the rest of the night. Some – not the players – abused his generosity by ordering bottles, rather than glasses, of champagne and whisky. Nicola woke up the next morning in a panic; she had left her credit card behind the bar and had visions of an enormous bill – but that, like everything else, had been settled by Keith.

I had that summer off because Wales only had a development tour and I resolved to get myself into shape for the new season because I wanted to renew my contract with Northampton at the end of it. The club arranged training sessions for the players who were over 30, but I opted out of those and worked alongside the younger players, pushing myself to the limit. It is not about how old you are, but how you feel, and the fact that I was not shown up by the youngsters proved to me that my career was nowhere near its end. I volunteered to play in the Middlesex Sevens a couple of weeks before the start of the season, along with the club's other internationals, but most of them pulled out when the time came. We made it to the semi-finals before Saracens knocked us out. It was a good way to prepare for the new campaign.

It was always going to be hard to follow up our success of the previous season, and we started both the league and the Heineken Cup badly. We had picked up a number of injuries and John's new gameplan needed time to come to terms with, but there is nothing like a few defeats to get you to return to the way you know. As the number one seeds in the Heineken Cup, we had a group which should have held no horrors for us: Edinburgh, Leinster and Biarritz. We lost our first match to Edinburgh at home to a late drop goal. Whereas the previous season things had gone for us in tight moments, the pendulum had now swung the other way. We only won one match in our group and were one of the first teams to be eliminated. This was the curse of the Heineken Cup: no team had ever successfully defended the trophy. The champions before us, Ulster, went through the following season without winning a group match.

We eventually got our game together after Christmas. Pat was sidelined after a shoulder operation and Tim Rodber, in his last season before retirement, took over the captaincy. He had led the club before and I was warned that he would be very serious and a hard taskmaster. He turned out to be laid-back, chatty and congenial. We finished fourth in the league, ensuring that the club would be in the Heineken Cup the following season and we had a home draw against Saracens in the inaugural championship play-offs in Zurich. We gave them a 12-point start, but then romped away with it, giving us three victories that season over a team we had regarded as a jinx. We faced the champions Leicester in the semi-final at Welford Road and we felt we had an excellent chance of winning because Leicester had already reached the Heineken Cup final and we hoped they would have their minds on other matters. Hope, though, is never enough against Leicester.

It turned out to be my 51st and final match for Northampton and I could not have gone out on a lower note. I got into a bad position and allowed myself to be handed off by their full-back Tim Stimpson in a move which led to a try. I had my poorest game for a while. It ended for me shortly before the hour when I injured my ankle in a tackle. I was in agony and thought I had done some major damage which would rule me out of Wales's tour to Japan that summer and perhaps even delay my return to Neath colours. Thankfully, the damage was minor and my main pain was the knowledge that I had let the team down. As I was leaving the field, I was given a wonderful ovation by the Leicester crowd in what could have been my final match in England, and that meant a lot.

We had been handicapped against Leicester by the absence through injury of our New Zealand flanker Andrew Blowers. He had broken his nose in a training accident three days before the semi-final. We had an opposed training session with the team chosen to play at Welford Road taking on the rest of the squad. It was meant to be full contact and no holding back. Blowers went in with the ball and the second row John Phillips prevented its release. As he did so, three players came in with their forearms to smash him out of the way. Phillips saw them and ducked; Blowers was not so fortunate and suddenly there was blood everywhere as he had his nose flattened against his face. Blowers was crucial to our game with his ability to keep moves alive and with his reading of the game. John Steele tried to persuade him to play, but Pat Lam told Blowers to see sense.

I had agreed to join Neath the previous March. I had spoken to John Steele before Christmas about a new contract and he said he needed more time to think about it. John Leslie, the Scotland centre, had just joined the club and he and I were expected to complement each other in the midfield. The signing of John meant that Matt Allen, an excellent player, would be marginalized and I felt that Steele would want me around the following season. I told him that I would see him at the end of January and in the meantime would talk to other clubs but not make a decision until we had met then. I spoke to him after Wales had played England at the beginning of February. I told him that a couple of clubs had approached me and he wanted to know if I had had an ultimatum. When I said no, he replied: 'If they are not in a rush, neither are we.' If he had offered me a one-year contract there and then I would have accepted it: moving would have meant taking Naomi out of school again and Nicola, who had always been totally supportive of me, would have had to have changed her job once more. We agreed as a family that I would only join another club if they offered me a two-year deal because it was not worth all the upheaval just for one.

On St David's Day, 1 March, I met Lyn Jones and agreed a two-year contract with Neath. I was driving back home when John Steele rang: he said he was in a position to offer me something. I said nothing to him, but I went in to the club the following day and told him that I was going back to Neath. He said he was disappointed because John Leslie and I had been playing well together, but I had given my word to Neath and there was no going back; the one-year offer had come too late. I could understand John's position, but he had not given me any indication of what he was thinking and I had presumed that because Pat Lam was not wanted, I too would be on my way.

While I was excited about the prospect of returning to Neath and Wales, I would gladly have stayed at Northampton. The club was all I had hoped that it would be and I will never forget my times there. The crowd always gave me their full support and, unusually these days, they were always generous to the opposition. I would like to go back there with Neath for a final farewell, but that means qualifying for the 2002–03 Heineken Cup. I was there when the Saints went marching in to collect a trophy for the first time in their long history and I will always have the medal to prove it.

FIFTEEN

SIMPLY THE BEST

Sitting down to pick your dream team can turn out to be a nightmare. Confining yourself to players you have appeared alongside and against does not make it easier. You want to choose guys who are your friends and objectivity can be elusive. I would not consider choosing the Australian David Campese on the wing, great player though he undoubtedly was, because he never showed any grace in defeat. After he handed the 1989 series to the Lions at the Sydney Football Stadium by throwing out a suicidal pass close to his own line, he chose to lambast the Lions for a gameplan which did not meet with his full approval rather than face up to his own mistake. Campese never missed an opportunity to rubbish England and I have never had much respect for players who place themselves above the game as Campese did.

Another problem with my dream team is that I played both codes of rugby. Do you pick 13 players or 15? It does not really matter among the backs, but the games are totally different for forwards. League second-rows like Bradley Clyde were outstanding, but there is no way he would have played in that position in union because of the set-piece demands that locks face; and the same goes for front-rowers – so picking a team of 15 means it is going to be biased in favour of rugby union. I am often asked which of the codes I most prefer, but it is not a relevant question. I enjoyed my time in rugby league, especially my first three years with Warrington and my stint with Cronulla, but I have played union for most of my life. They are different games and it is not a case of one being better than the other. Theories have been advanced that there will be a merger of the two but not only can I not see that happening, but I do not think it should happen. There is a lot the codes can learn from each other. Since going professional union has taken some league ideas on board, like the sin bin and the video referee, but they are as distinct as cricket and baseball and while the ending of the cold war between the two sets of governing bodies was welcome, that should be as far as it goes.

Rugby union has changed considerably since I started with Maesteg in 1984. Professionalism has made a big difference, but countries like Australia and New Zealand were professional in terms of attitude long before 1995. The game is much faster today and the ball-in-play time is virtually double what it was 15 years ago. It means you are far more involved as a player, even if you are a wing, and huge strides have been made in terms of fitness and conditioning.

The game is far more scientific today, and if it means that players of the genius of Barry John and Phil Bennett are rarely seen, the upside is that there is now an increased emphasis on athleticism and if you are one-dimensional, the chances are that you will not get very far. The game is about teams rather than individuals, and if that is upsetting to the romantics, it has allowed players like me to flourish. In the days when teams only trained two evenings a week and there were far more matches than there are now, there used to be a lot of aimless play with forwards often treating a game as an excuse to settle old scores while the backs stood idly by.

Full-back is a position which sums up how much union has changed. Full-backs used to be seen as the last line of defence, summed up by J.P.R. Williams of Bridgend and Wales whose tackling became legendary. Williams scored more tries than any of his predecessors, but at a time when the ball was kicked away more than now, his ability under the high ball and his rock-like solidity were more valuable. Fast-forward to the 2001 Six Nations and you have players like Iain Balshaw, Rhys Williams and Chris Paterson strutting their stuff at full-back, players with little in common with J.P.R. They all had the pace of wings (Balshaw's position with his club Bath), and they were chosen despite question marks about their defence –

Balshaw in particular. Defences in rugby union are now so well organised anyway that full-backs are far better protected than they were.

The best full-back that I have seen was the Australian rugby league player Darren Lockyer. He had everything and like so many of his countrymen, he allied natural ability with a physical and mental hardness. In union, New Zealand's Christian Cullen is the best example of an attacking full-back, and it was hard to understand when the All Blacks started to play him in the centre in the 1999 World Cup. When we played New Zealand at Wembley in 1997, we set out to contain Jonah Lomu on the left wing and it worked in the sense that the big man did not score a try. Our attention to him left gaps, though, which Cullen all too ably exploited and he claimed a hat-trick of tries. He had the pace to exploit space and the vision to see it and he quickly set a try-scoring record for a New Zealand full-back.

Lomu would be one of my wings. I had never seen a wing like him: he was not just big, weighing in at around 18 st, but he was as quick as anyone around and it was that unprecedented combination of power and speed that took teams in the 1995 World Cup by surprise. Lomu can be suspect in defence; he is slow to turn and sometimes fumbles the ball on the floor, but he is the player in the game most likely to empty bars and he does not overplay his hand. He is a great team player and if his presence creates space for others, he is never reluctant to exploit it. He turned from someone few had heard of into a world superstar in the space of a few weeks in 1995, but fame has not affected him and there is no danger of his burning out early in the manner of some other sporting heroes.

On the other wing, I would go for Ieuan Evans of Wales and the Lions. He had the misfortune that for most of his career Wales were a struggling team. Even so, he created a new try-scoring record and went on three tours with the Lions. He was not the biggest wing, but he had a deceptive strength and as a finisher he was in a class of his own. He led Wales with distinction for four years and was unfortunate to be relieved of the captaincy before the 1995 World Cup. He would probably have won 100 caps for Wales but for a succession of injuries, but he retained his pace to the end and proved with the Lions that he could keep illustrious company. He was a true competitor who tackled more than his weight and he was one of the best players ever produced by Wales.

I have already gone for the Australian rugby league pair Laurie Daley and Andrew Ettingshausen in the centre of my dream team. Jeremy Guscott and Scott Gibbs would be my union pair, for their combination of strength and stealth. Good centres come in pairs: Jason Little and Tim Horan of Australia; Jeremy Guscott and Will Carling for England; Mark Taylor and Scott Gibbs for Wales; Joe Stanley and later Frank Bunce and Walter Little for New Zealand – and by 2001, Brian O'Driscoll and Rob Henderson had established themselves as an effective combination for Ireland. Jonathan Davies is renowned as an outside-half in union, but he made a superb centre in league: one step ahead of the game and a player of such talent that he was the ultimate match-winner.

At outside-half, I would go not for Jonathan Davies but Neil Jenkins. Neil is a player who has spent virtually his entire career with Wales, taking an unseemly amount of criticism. He has been my hero in the time I have been playing, a players' player who is not just an incredibly consistent goal-kicker but who brings out the best in those around him. His achievements should speak for themselves: the first player in the history of international rugby to reach 1,000 points, the most-capped Wales player ever – and he has scored more than 100 tries in his career. I have been on the same field as other great outside-halves, including Jonathan Davies, Grant Fox, Andrew Mehrtens, Michael Lynagh and Jonny Wilkinson, but I would go for Neil every time. Despite all that he has done, he has been unaffected by fame and is as modest now as he was when he started his career. When he retires from international rugby, he will be sorely missed and that is the time when his greatness will be fully appreciated.

My scrum-half would be another Welshman: Robert Jones. He was a gutsy player with great hands. Like Ieuan, he had the misfortune to play for Wales in a period of decline, but he was a key player for the Lions in Australia in 1989 when he took on Nick Farr-Jones. Their confrontation early in the second Test, when Robert squared up to the Australian despite conceding a few inches in height, was a psychological turning point after the Lions had gone 1–0 down in the series. Farr-Jones was a great player. Joost van der Westhuizen was the world's leading scrum-half for a while and I rate Rob Howley who will probably top Robert Jones' achievements, but to me Robert had it all as a scrum-half. He was not the biggest player, but he was effective in everything he did and he had that touch of class which made him stand out from the rest.

The front row is pretty much a mystery to me and, I suspect, to most who do not practise its art. Props and hookers live in their own world and I will remain eternally grateful that no coach ever decided that I should be part of that nether land. My hooker would be Kevin Phillips, who played for Wales and for Neath in my first spell there. He had incredible powers of motivation and never knew when he was beaten. He might not have been the best hooker in terms of the set-piece, but he pioneered the quickly taken penalty. He used to be criticised for tapping and going when he played for Wales, but what Kevin did then, others followed seven or eight years later, recognising the value of running at a disorganised defence. His reputation suffered when Ron Waldron's Neath experiment with Wales failed, but he was a key player at the Gnoll who was of undoubted international quality. He was ahead of his time and he would fit in comfortably to the modern game.

My props would be Brian Williams, of Neath and Wales, and the South African Gary Pagel who was with me at Northampton. Brian weighed little more than me and he looked anything but a prop. He played for Wales under Ron, but the step up came late in his career and he was discovered in the scrum. I will remember him from my days at Neath – a forward who was like an extra flanker on the loose, popping up everywhere; a player of such strength that he could rob anybody in a maul. He packed a mean punch, too, and like Kevin Phillips he was a West Wales farmer who had a natural strength. He was quiet and unassuming off the field, but on it he was one of the most influential players of his generation. Gary was virtually the opposite of Brian: a powerful scrummager who never took a step backwards. He played for Northampton in his twilight years, and at his peak he must have been some prop. As with centres, props come in pairs in today's game. Brian and Gary would provide the essential combination of tight and loose and they were two of the hardest players that I have ever come across. David Young was a tight-head out of the top drawer, a Lion in 1989, 1997 and 2001 who, unusually for a front-rower, made a successful conversion to rugby league. I think he liked having me in the Wales squad because it meant he was not the oldest player!

Second-row forwards also come in twos. My front jumper would be England's Martin Johnson, the captain of the Lions in 1997 and 2001. He is a player who does not use words liberally, but he leads by example and in South Africa he proved a perfect buffer between the players and the management. He played in New Zealand in his formative years and there is every chance that if he had decided to stay there, he would have been capped by the All Blacks. He had to have been the only choice to lead the Lions again, not just because of what he had achieved with Leicester and England in the intervening four years, but because he is a player others look up to and opponents respect. He is old-fashioned in the sense that he does not take any messing and even in the 2001 Heineken Cup final he had ten minutes in the sin bin after throwing a couple of punches at an opponent who was committing a professional foul. He is not, though, a dirty forward in the sense that he goes around starting trouble. He merely lets anyone know if they step out of line.

I would pair the Australian John Eales with Martin Johnson. Eales is one of the tallest players in the game but is also one of the most athletic. He kicks goals, lands drop-shots from the halfway line and is as quick around the field as a back-rower. Lomu was described as a freak during the 1995 World Cup, but Eales also broke the mould because second-rows of his height were usually useful in the tight but nowhere else. New Zealand's Ian Jones was another multi-dimensional lock. He did not have Eales's height, but he would dominate a lineout and would often appear on the wing in broken play. When he started, the All Blacks did not place a high value on entertainment, but Jones became a fixture for the Barbarians and he revelled in the freedom of exhibition matches. Chris Wyatt of Wales had a raw ability that Graham Henry managed to refine for a year or two before losing patience with the player's individualism. You have to conform to a large degree these days with organisation, an important feature of any side, and it is becoming harder and harder for mavericks to survive. They have to be, like Campese was, far better than any of their rivals.

In the back row, I would have Lawrence Dallaglio at blind-side flanker. Another important figure in South Africa in 1997, he would walk into a World XV. When I was at Richmond and Northampton, Wasps without Dallaglio lacked sting; it was not quite a case of one man making a team but it was as near to it as you will get. In the 2001 Zurich Championship play-off between Wasps and Bath at Loftus Road, Wasps were leading at half-time when Dallaglio was forced off by a knee injury. Bath then took charge and made it to the final. Had Dallaglio remained on the field, Wasps would probably not have lost. He had to reinvent himself after a series of allegations about him were made in a newspaper in the summer of 1999. He was stripped of the England captaincy and he faced being banned from the game, but he had the strength of character to re-emerge an even stronger character than before. As a captain, he will not count Wembley 1999 as one of his greatest days. England had been in charge of the match virtually throughout and they had the chance to nail the victory with a penalty eight minutes from time. Dallaglio chose to go for a kick to touch and a driving lineout, remembering no doubt that that was how the game against Wales at Twickenham the previous year had turned. Lightning did not strike twice and Scott Gibbs, a close friend of Dallaglio's, rubbed it in with his try in the final minute.

On the open-side, I have seen a number of outstanding players – Josh Kronfeld, David Wilson, Neil Back, Ruben Kruger, Gwyn Jones, Budge Pountney and Peter Winterbottom among them – but the player I would choose is the Frenchman Laurent Cabannes. He was at Richmond with me and had an uncanny knack of appearing in the right place at the right time. He had the skills of a three-quarter, but he was a typical French forward in that he liked the graft and the confrontation that the tight exchanges provided. French rugby is often a mixture of beauty and brutality, and although Cabannes could hardly be described as a thug, he knew how to look after himself. His real strength came when the ball was moved wide and his hands (a feature that let players like Josh Kronfeld and Andrew Blowers down) were sure. He rarely made a mistake and of all the overseas signings made by Richmond, he was the best.

I would go for rugby league's Ellery Hanley at number 8, along with Scott Quinnell; one half each. One of the greatest footballers of any era, a place has to be found for Hanley somewhere. He could probably play anywhere in the three-quarters, but it is as a forward that I remember him. Had he played union, he would have been a natural. Scott is a forward I have the highest regard for. He was outstanding for the Lions in Australia 2001 and is a player like Neil Jenkins whose real value to Wales will only be properly appreciated when he retires. Zinzan Brooke was the most skilful number 8 that I ever saw, but he could be a pig of a man and I would not want him in my team. After Wales had played New Zealand in 1997, one of the players went up to Brooke and asked if he would swap jerseys. Brooke looked at him and said contemptuously: 'What would I want your jersey for? I would not wipe my backside with it.' It was an appalling remark, unbecoming of a leading player in one of the best teams in the world. New Zealand have come to appreciate the meaning of the word humility since: number 8s did not come any more humble than the great Gary Teichmann.

International rugby is now getting to the stage where some players play almost as much for their country in a season as they do for their club. When I was first capped by Wales in 1990, national squad sessions were often arranged ad hoc. Teams were not allowed to gather in a hotel together more than 48 hours before an international. As these were all played on a Saturday it meant you would train with Wales on Monday and Wednesday afternoons and assemble on Thursday. There are no restrictions now though, and the week of an international starts on a Sunday when we assemble at a hotel in the Vale of Glamorgan at 5 p.m. We have some dinner before having a team meeting that lasts for between one and two hours during which Graham Henry outlines how the week will go.

Players do not have to stay in the hotel between Sunday and Thursday and are free to return home at nights if they wish. I never did this because Northampton was too far away, but those who do decide not to stay have to report for duty each morning promptly otherwise they face being fined. Monday starts at 10 a.m. when we have a two-hour session based largely on attacking from lineouts. After lunch, we work on attacking from scrums and go through our range of moves which are all drawn up by Henry. When he arrived, he ripped up all the old moves and introduced his own, more than 60 of them, and you have to practise and practise at them. There is no short cut. We have a hard base of ten moves which do not change from game to game with Henry introducing one or two new ones from time to time to make sure that opponents are kept guessing.

Tuesday is the hardest day of the week. It is not unusual for a number of players to sit out the Monday session because of knocks they have picked up in club matches during the weekend – one of the reasons why Henry is so keen on keeping the squad together for the duration of the Six Nations. You can pick up injuries in training too, especially on a Tuesday when we have a two-hour defensive session. Henry often invites teams, like Pontypridd, Cardiff or Neath, down and in the afternoon we go indoors to work on defensive organisation. It is a day that takes it out of you. On Wednesday there is just one session during which we work on our phase play and restarts. Players have that afternoon and evening off, reassembling the following evening.

Friday is a light day when we have what we call 'the captain's walk-through', turning up at the match venue and going through a few lineouts and scrums. It amounts to nothing more than limbering up and it is the time when the nerves start. Some players start getting quiet, as you stand in an empty stadium knowing that in little more than 24 hours it is going to be packed out. The captain will meet with the players that evening and make a speech which usually lasts around 30 minutes. He will go through the gameplan and tell each player individually what is expected of him. Alun Carter, the former Wales flanker who is now the squad's video analyst, then shows a tape of the players which is designed to motivate, highlighting your best displays and moments.

The week sometimes drags and it is a relief when Saturday comes. We go out to the cinema or try our hand at ten-pin bowling, but you are only too aware that these diversions are an attempt to make time pass. I started reading books again after returning to the Wales squad.

There is hardly ever anything on television and going on to the internet is expensive because of the telephone rates charged by hotels. There is no stated bedtime and you are left to your own devices outside the timetable laid down by the coach. They do not keep tabs on you and there is a strong element of trust. You justify your place through your performances and if players have a lifestyle Henry is not happy with, they will have no problems just as long as they train hard and play well. The players have ruled that there will be no alcohol in the week before a match. Whether everyone sticks to this, who knows – but a decree coming from players rather than the management is more likely to be observed.

I usually get up at 10.15 on a Saturday morning, as late as I can. I follow the same routine that I do at home: a bowl of Corn Flakes with full-cream milk and some coffee. I had a problem when we first moved to the hotel in the Vale because they only had semi-skimmed milk and I could not stand that. It got to the stage where I brought my own milk, having cleared it with the dietician. I have three or four cups of coffee, making sure that my final one is no less than three hours before kick-off otherwise I end up going to the loo all the time. I get nervous as the start of the game approaches, even if I am only on the bench. It is something that age and experience have not improved in me. You are so hydrated during the week, as you're told to take water on board at every opportunity, that coffee goes straight through you and there have been times when I have visited the loo 20 times in the last 60 minutes before a game starts. Players are often seen drinking water at the start of games, even when the weather is bitterly cold. This is usually because they are washing their mouthguards, which dry the mouth horribly. I never wore a mouthguard until I came back from rugby league, but since an incident when I had a cap knocked out I have worn one religiously. I played for Wales against Romania in 1997 and had a tooth come loose after I was smashed in the face. I was told to get a mouthguard then and was sent to a dentist. It was uncomfortable at first but it quickly became a habit. Some players would not take the field without a scrum cap but I am too old for that.

After breakfast on Saturday, the forwards get together to go through their lineout routines and the backs have a gentle jog. Food is served after noon – sandwiches or pasta. We then meet and get on the coach at around 1 p.m. for the drive to the ground. We often get a police escort when we are away from home, and it helps the players relax when they see traffic cops in Paris and Rome kicking the doors of cars that are slowing us down. In Britain, we have to queue quietly and observe red lights, but the drive from the Vale to the Millennium Stadium is not long and we are always at the ground at least 90 minutes before kick-off. We have our final team meeting just before we leave the hotel. Graham Henry gives an address, sometimes going through all the players and the bench individually saying what he expects, and sometimes giving his general view of the way we should approach the game.

I am not one for team-talks, having heard it all before, but as one of the more seasoned players in the squad I am expected to contribute. Four years ago, I never said a thing but now I pipe up and go through what I think is important. I am not sure that anyone really listens because as the minutes tick by, players become locked into their own world. We warm up 30 minutes before the game and then it is back to the dressing-room where the captain has the final say after the referee has given us the five-minute warning. Rob Howley and David Young were both excellent communicators. They knew the game inside out and would always make sound points. The captaincy did affect Rob's form, not least because the games came thick and fast for him by the end. I was not surprised when Henry took the captaincy off him, but I was astounded when he was dropped from the side. Even when he was not operating at 100 per cent, he was still by some way the best scrum-half in Wales. But what do I know? We won the two matches that Rob sat out and when he came back the following season, he had his zest and snap of old. There were suggestions that Rob was dropped after having refused to make the captain's speech at the after-match dinner at Twickenham. David Young, now captain, was not at the function because he was resting a calf injury, but Rob had every right to turn Henry's request down having been dumped as captain and it was insensitive to ask him.

After-match dinners are one of the banes of international rugby.

You want to get out and enjoy yourself with your team-mates and, sometimes, the opposition – and you find yourself on a table in a huge hall, uncomfortably dressed in a dinner jacket as an old amateur ritual is lived out. Time should be called on these expensive bashes. A finger buffet immediately after a match to which wives and girlfriends were invited would not only save money but it would give players the chance to relax properly in the evening. The functions often drag on until midnight and what can you do then?

After Twickenham in 2000, Henry was so furious with the performance that he imposed a 2 a.m. curfew when players had not just to be back in the hotel but also safely tucked up in bed. He called a team meeting the following morning. He had heard that some players had been up until at least 4 a.m. drinking in the hotel bar and he wanted to know who they were. There was silence for a while until the prop Peter Rogers slowly stuck up his hand.

'Er, I was in bed by 3.45 a.m., Graham. I know because I looked at my watch.'

Sniggers followed and a few more hands went up. Henry said nothing and left the room. I suspect he had ordered the clampdown because of an incident the previous month after Ireland had been trounced by England at Twickenham. One of the Irish players had got into an altercation with an angry fan in the early hours of the Sunday morning. The supporter was upset that the players were drinking and enjoying themselves after what he considered to be a humiliating defeat – but win or lose you have to get it out of your system, and the morning after Twickenham, we were put through a training session. Everyone turned up, but most in body rather than spirit.

This was not Henry's finest hour because the Grannygate saga was about to explode in his face. The drawbridge was drawn up and, for the first time in his reign, we were discouraged from speaking to the press. We had to look inwards and draw strength from each other. It is often said that players do not read newspapers, but they do – not least because they invariably supply ammunition to tease other players with, after absurd comments have been made and unwise picture shoots agreed to. Few actively court publicity and some are more comfortable answering questions than others. We are not coached what to say, but everyone is made aware of what something said in an unguarded moment (like 'Shane Who?') may generate in terms of headlines.

Humour is important and when Garin Jenkins and David Young were both in the Wales squad, they bounced one-liners off each other; two men, each with a very quick wit which I envied. Rugby is about more than just the playing: it is about fitting in and I am fortunate that there are very few players over the years that I have not got on with.

SIXTEEN

ALL IN THE MIND

'You are only as young as the woman you feel,' an American comedian once said. In rugby terms, you are only as young as the opposite number you manage to get the better of. As I approach my 37th birthday, the subject of my age is often thrown at me: 'How long can you expect to carry on?' 'Is it not time you packed it in?' But why should I be judged on my age rather than my performance? There were mutterings that my being chosen for Wales's summer tour of Japan in 2001 was sending out the wrong message and that I was going along almost as a 'thank you', denying a younger player the chance to prove himself and gain some experience. It was an argument which did not hold water. Sentiment had nothing to do with my selection and if I was good enough to appear in a championship play-off for Northampton shortly after the Wales squad was announced, why was I not worth a place in a 38-strong party? I had no intention of going out there just to make up the numbers and enjoy myself; with Mark Taylor in Australia with the Lions, there was a Test place to be claimed.

One answer was that I would not be around for the 2003 World Cup. In the autumn of 2001, I became the oldest centre to appear for Wales and had no intention of retiring from international rugby, but when Graham Henry resigned as the Wales coach after the opening weekend of the 2002 Six Nations, his successor Steve Hansen called me in and said that he was going to give younger players the chance.

He was not saying that I would never be considered for international rugby again, but his message was clear: only a spate of injuries would put me in contention again and he asked me to act as mentor to Cardiff's promising young centre, Jamie Robinson, a role I was only too pleased to take on.

I appreciated Steve's honesty and he was right to look ahead, but I felt I still had something to offer. I had held down my place in a successful Neath side, but Wales had struggled in the autumn internationals. We were routed at home by Ireland in the rearranged Six Nations match and it was comfortably my worst appearance in an international jersey: we had a collective off-day and all wanted the chance to redeem ourselves, but the performance in the following match against Argentina was little better and the pressure grew on Graham. He had suffered intense criticism during and after the Lions tour to Australia, and while I do not think that undermined his position, even though some Welsh players felt hard done by, the experience did affect him. Scott Gibbs retired from international rugby, followed by David Young, while Neil Jenkins was injured. A hard core of experienced players, who had performed well for Graham, was lost and rebuilding had to be done two years before the World Cup.

Graham brought Hansen on board to provide a new face and a different outlook, but though we pushed Australia all the way in Cardiff at the end of November 2001, Ireland put 54 points on us in Dublin at the start of the championship campaign and Graham decided to stand down. It was a sad end to what had been a fulfilling time with his adopted country: people tended to forget what it had been like before Graham, but his approach to the job, not afraid to get involved on the political side, meant he made enemies. He never missed the opportunity to say how he thought the game should be structured and he was happy to put himself in the firing line with the media. Hansen is a different character, a players' man who regards the media as an occupational hazard. Results did not happen for him immediately, but Wales came closest to beating the eventual Grand Slam winners, France, and they could, and probably should, have won their two Tests on the summer tour to South Africa.

It had been 11 years since I had played in Wales and a lot had changed. The season had only just started when six of the clubs in the top division launched a campaign to have Neath, Ebbw Vale and Caerphilly dumped out of the top flight. Their argument was that there was only enough money in the game to fund six professional sides, but appointing themselves to the elite was never going to be popular. Neath was excluded because we were run by a company which was owned by the Welsh Rugby Union, but we showed that in rugby terms we were among the best in Wales by finishing in the top four of the Welsh–Scottish league. Had we won our final match at Swansea, we would have been champions but the pressure got to us and we lost 20–16, paving the way for Llanelli to clinch the title a few days later at Cardiff, but we had achieved our objective of qualifying for the Heineken Cup. I was on the bench for the Swansea match and finished the season playing a one-off game for Ebbw Vale on loan.

I have one year to run on my contract with Neath and I will be 38 when it ends. As long as I am fit and proving my worth in the squad, I would consider carrying on, but sport does not offer a secure future and I was delighted when I got a job again in the haematology department at Morriston Hospital.

The trouble with sport is that ageism is rife: players pass 30 and suddenly they start feeling old because of what they hear and read. Sir Stanley Matthews was still playing soccer when he was 50, and even if I do not expect to be lacing up my boots at that age, I will only consider retiring when I feel that I am not up to it. No one will need to tell me. When the time comes that I cannot beat a defender on the outside or when runners are breaking my tackles, I will know that my day has come and I will not be like a boxer who takes on one fight too many. I want to go out with my reputation intact and not be seen as some sad old case who was unable to read the writing on the wall.

When I signed a two-year contract with Neath, I was not interested in the security aspect of the deal. I told them that if I struggled in my first season with them, I would not hold them to the agreement and take easy money, not just because the club means so much to me, but because I would not do that to anyone. I would not be interested in just turning up for training and getting the occasional appearance if someone was injured, marginalised to the point where I was being shown the door marked 'exit'. I knew when I joined Neath that I would have to fight for my place. James Storey is an outside-centre with a big future; he was voted man of the match in the 2001 Principality Cup final even though Neath lost to Newport, and I would not stand in his way if I felt that I was not at least his equal.

There has been an assumption that I will end up taking a coaching role at Neath, but that is not something I have given any thought to. My priority is to concentrate on playing and when I do eventually retire, I may step away from the game. I have always thrived on organising defences and I like thinking about the game, but it is totally different when you are on the field to when you are stuck in a dug-out, and just because you have been successful as a player does not mean you will make it as a coach. Graham Henry is one of the best coaches I have played under, but he never appeared for the All Blacks. He has an innate understanding of the game and that, coupled with his ability to get it across to the players in a direct but non-patronising manner, makes him stand out from most of the rest. I am not sure if I would have the necessary communication skills to make my mark as a coach.

I am far more interested in the fitness side of things and have spent a lot of time talking to the Wales fitness coach, Peter Herbert. When I do stop playing, there is no way I will let my fitness go. I relish going on long runs and doing endurance work. I believe that my career has gone on for so long principally because I have never let myself go. There would be one drawback to becoming a fitness coach, though: I could hardly go on to players about the need to watch their diet as a consumer of chips, full-cream milk and various other goodies that are on the dietician's list of what not to eat. I have a leaning towards science, and conditioning would interest me more than rugby. I would not be into the motivation side of things, like Steve Black, but would be more into measuring how players are doing because when it comes to fitness, there are no short cuts.

My career has astounded me. My passing is limited, I cannot kick the ball out of hand, my ball skills are average and I have had to work hard on my game to make up for the natural ability that I lack. This is probably why I have managed to achieve so much without being a 'tall poppy', there to be knocked down by all and sundry. I suppose I have been like a batsman in cricket who goes about his task stealthily, reaching 70 or 80 without his opponents, or the crowd, realising it. I had won 35 caps for Wales by the end of the 2001–02 season, and, considering I did not win my fifth until I was a couple of months away from my 32nd birthday, I regard that as an achievement – I won 31 caps between the ages of 32 and 36 and there are not many players in the history of the game who have matched that. I may have won many more had I not joined Warrington in 1990, but equally I could have become a victim of the backlash against Neath when Ron Waldron resigned as national coach. You can speculate all you like, but you will never know.

If I had the chance to change one thing in my career, the answer would be turning Warrington down and staying with Neath, not because I didn't enjoy my time at Warrington but because I missed out on the things happening at Neath. But it was only by going to rugby league that I got the experience of playing in Australia and then in England. Had I remained in Wales, I have no doubt that I would have seen out my career there and that I would not have gone on much beyond the 1995 World Cup. I did not appreciate it then, but there is wanderlust in me which kicks in every couple of years. I was wrong to sign for Warrington for five years; that was far too long and I would not make that mistake again, but one of the highlights of my career was playing for Cronulla. I wanted to find out whether I could compete at that level and it was unfortunate that Nicola and I had to leave Sydney a year earlier than we had intended to.

Another thing I would change is going back to Maesteg after they had rejected me. I wanted to play for them out of a sense of loyalty and I eventually had four happy years at the Old Parish, but I would have been better off, in a rugby sense, had I joined Neath instead of taking a year off with Maesteg Celtic. I dropped down the pecking order as far as the national squad was concerned, and if Ron Waldron had not become Wales coach it is possible that my Wales career would never have started, that Warrington would not have been tempted to move in for me, and that I would have simply become a club hack in Wales. Maesteg will always mean a lot to me, but among the things I have learned in my career is that you have to look after yourself because no one else will.

One aspect I will not miss having moved back to Wales is the driving to and from national training sessions. My Wales colleagues would argue that I am not the safest driver on the road but this is something I would dispute: it is just that accidents tend to happen to me before Wales play England. I was driving to training once four years ago and when I was near Monmouth on a dual carriageway, I went through a puddle, the car spun round and ended up smashing into the central reservation. It was a write-off but somehow I pulled myself from the wreckage without a scratch. The following year, I met Jonathan Davies one day in Llandaff. The Wales squad was leaving for London the following day, but when I went back to my car, a window had been smashed and the radio stolen. I had to wait up until 3 a.m. for the damage to be repaired. A 60–26 defeat by England was to follow.

The worst incident, though, occurred before the international against Samoa in November 2000. I was driving to Heathrow Airport to pick up Nicola. There was a build-up of traffic and a lot of stop-starting. I was trying to read a map at the same time as shuffling forward in the queue when I looked up and realised I was going to hit the car in front. I spun the wheel and shot out into the road, fortunate that nothing was coming towards me because that would have been the end. I crashed into a sign and ended up picking up a bill for £6,500 damages. It could have been a lot worse.

When someone reaches the age of 100, they get a telegram from the Queen and are asked by reporters what the secret is to their long innings. The usual replies are to do with not smoking and not drinking to excess, but there is probably no one factor. I have no real idea why I have been able to play at the top level for so long. Most of the players who started out at the same time as me have long since retired, but the likes of Owain Williams, Kevin Ellis, Rowland Phillips, Mark Jones and Paul Moriarty were still playing top-division rugby in Wales in 2000–01. I suppose my longevity is unusual because I am a three-quarter; in that position, when your speed goes, so do your friends. Forwards can get away with slowing down to a trundle, even today, but not centres or wings.

Survival is a mental battle. I largely eat and drink what I want, but I have never let my fitness slip. I have been fortunate never to suffer a serious injury. I have had the usual wear and tear and my hamstrings have regularly played up, but I have never been out of the game for a long period of time. I have had two hernia operations, as well as surgery on a knee, a shoulder and my nose, but I've always recovered quickly. My secret formula was to rest for a few days and then have a couple of nights on the beer. It always did the trick, even if medical experts advised against it. No one knows one's body better than oneself and I have never taken supplements to aid recovery; the healing process has always been natural.

Having a job outside rugby for the first 11 years of my career also helped prolong my career. I worked at Morriston Hospital in Swansea, Booth Hall Children's Hospital in Manchester, Kerfoot Pharmaceuticals in Denton, Acer Environment in Runcorn and St George's Medical Centre in Sydney. When I joined Richmond in 1996, it was impossible to get another job because of my training commitments and it was the same at Northampton, but Neath only train in the mornings and I will be looking to ease myself back into haematology work by taking a refresher course. I suppose this is ironic given that the prime reason I left Neath in 1990 was because I felt I was being stretched to the limit by the demands of rugby and work. The difference in those days, though, was that you were not paid for playing rugby.

It was also ironic that when I was in Australia, I was putting in more hours off the field than I had done when I was at Neath. After I had been in Sydney for a few months, I went to the hospital and asked if I could have a look round the pathology department. I was offered a job there and then and did not hesitate in saying yes. I would clock on at 6.30 a.m. and work a 12-hour shift before going to train with Cronulla or play – matches started at 8.30 p.m. I thought at the time that I probably had a couple of years left in me as a player and that I needed to sort out what I was going to do when I retired. I did well at St George's and was offered the job of lab manager. I would have taken it and committed myself to staying in Australia for the medium-term, but we took the decision to return to Britain and the chance was lost.

I have been fortunate to have had a very supportive wife in Nicola. I have known her ever since I started playing rugby, and but for her I would probably have packed in rugby after a couple of years at Maesteg because I was not getting anywhere. It was Nicola, together with our friends David and Debbie Chadwick, who spent hours and hours painstakingly putting together a video of my rugby league career to send to clubs in Australia – an act that landed me the contract with Cronulla and paved the way for the second phase of my career as a rugby union player. Nicola has had a successful career herself, she is a make-up artist who has worked in films and television.

I have also been fortunate in the coaches I have worked with, starting with Brian Nicholas at Maesteg and ending with Lyn Jones and Graham Henry. If I had to choose one as the best, it would be John Lang of Cronulla who later went on to coach the Australian rugby league side. Lang bubbled with ideas and had a revolutionary approach to the game. He would wind himself up into a frenzy because he would get so excited about something and he transmitted that enthusiasm to the players. He believed that rugby should be about fulfilment through enjoyment and enjoyment came from winning. Brian Johnson and Ron Waldron were great motivators and Clive Griffiths taught me a lot about defence. I have never failed to get on with a coach and they all have one thing in common: if you put in the effort for them, you will not have any problems. Professionalism is an overused word, but it boils down to putting rugby first. Your shelf-life as a player is short, and you will have many years to regret missed opportunities. I am happy that I have made the most of what nature blessed me with.

Above all, I am glad that I had the chance to play rugby union in the old days of amateurism, when there was a social side to the game that was the envy of other sports. Seasons always ended with a tour which we regarded as a reward in lieu of payment. Some of the behaviour left a lot to be desired and would not be tolerated today, though. When I was at Maesteg Youth, we played a match in West Wales against Whitland and stayed overnight. Someone was celebrating something and a fair amount of drink was consumed. The upshot was a mini-riot. Virtually every bedroom door was kicked in, a window in an adjacent nightclub was smashed, beds were kicked in two and one player locked himself in a police car and could not get out. The players had to contribute to a thousand-pound kitty to help pay for the damages and Maesteg Youth were banned from staying anywhere for three years. Whitland had let the Welsh Rugby Union know about what had gone on – so much for rugby's fraternity. It was not much better when I went to Arcachon with Wales B in 1989: there was a big party after the game and everything in the team-room was turned upside down with chairs and tables flying like in a Wild West movie. There was not too much damage, but there is no way things could get out of hand like that in the modern game.

Sports psychologists are now widely employed to ensure that nobody loses their head. Wales had one during the 1995 rugby league World Cup and he entered into the month-long drinking session with as much relish as the players. He would always turn up for his meetings with us with a big smile on his face. One of his ideas was to take the twice-removed Welshmen (the players from Wigan and other clubs who had rarely been to Wales) on to the National Stadium where they would plug in to Walkmans and have the national anthem blaring into their ears. He would tell them to close their eyes and take it all in, but all they really ended up with was earache.

At Richmond, we used to wind the sports psychologist up mercilessly. When Scott Quinnell joined Richmond, he had to leave his dog behind in Llanelli. The other Welsh players would tell the psychologist that Scott was depressed because he was missing his mutt and therapy would follow, with Scott playing along with the wind-up as the academic tried to help him come to terms with his grief. It was the same with John Davies, a farmer from West Wales. The psychologist was told that John had had to sell his cows and was suffering withdrawal symptoms. I played on the age factor: I said I felt I was too old to carry on and was getting fed up with the other players calling me granddad. He would question me and try to put my mind at rest, but I never suffered from any complex. We were out of order, I suppose, but sports psychology never did anything for me. I am not an emotional person and do not suffer from highs and lows: players with mood swings found the sessions more valuable but when I was asked to close my eyes and imagine a colour or the crowd at the Millennium Stadium, all I could see was black and white.

The most bizarre experience with a psychologist came just before the 1999 rugby union World Cup. The Wales squad were in North Wales and we were in a café by the top of Mount Snowdon. A sports psychologist from England, a Welshman, had sent in a tape-recording to help with our preparations and we found ourselves all crouching on the floor of the café listening to the tape which told us to relax, to think of all the great players who had appeared in a Wales jersey and to imagine running out on to the pitch of the Millennium Stadium for the start of the World Cup. It was meant to be a confidence booster, but we ended up lying there for some 45 minutes. I did not feel any better than I had done before, just a bit stiffer. I do not need any help to get myself prepared for matches. Northampton used a sports psychologist and he was the best one I came across because he did manage to generate enthusiasm, but it is a field where the subject needs to be receptive and I most definitely was not.

My mother was the most effective psychologist that I encountered. When I talked about playing for Manchester United and giving up rugby for soccer, Mum knew how to nudge me in the right direction: 'have no boots, will not travel anywhere'. Without her, I would doubtless have suffered the broken dreams of the vast majority of teenagers who think they have what it takes to make it in soccer only to find that the reality is different. I was brought up in a rugby environment and I understood the culture of the game whereas soccer was a different world. Mum's ultimatum was the making of me – little though I knew it then, as I pulled the longest of faces.

If anyone had told me when I was starting out with Maesteg that I would still be playing at the age of 37, I wouldn't just have not believed them, I would not have wanted to. When I told Gwyn Evans that I could not imagine myself playing at the age of 28, I meant it. Ten years seemed a lifetime then but it wasn't as if I was playing rugby because I thought I had to rather than because I wanted to; and now I am at the stage when I do not want my career to end. The Quinnell brothers and Barry Williams never stopped ribbing me in our Richmond days about my age – but that other Batman is still playing on television some 37 years after the series first came out, and the Caped Crusader does not look any older now than he did then. Here's to flying long and high.

STATISTICS

WALES

DATE	AGAINST	POSITION	SCORE	
1990:	Scotland (H)	Centre	L 9–13	
	Ireland (A)	Centre	L 8–14	
	Namibia (A)	Centre	W 18–9	
	Namibia (A)	Centre	W 34–30	
1996:	South Africa (H)	Centre	L 20–37	
1997:	United States (H)	Centre	W 34–14	
	Scotland (A)	Centre	W 34–19	
	France (A)	Centre	L 22–27	1 try
	England (H)	Centre	L 13–34	
	Romania (H)	Centre	W 70–21	2 tries
	New Zealand (H)	Centre	L 7–42	
1998:	Italy (H)	Centre	W 23–20	
	England (A)	Centre	L 26–60	2 tries
	Scotland (H)	Centre	W 19–13	
	Ireland (A)	Centre	W 30–21	1 try
1999:	Scotland (A)	Centre	L 20–33	
	Argentina (A)	Centre	W 36–26	
	Argentina (A)	Centre	W 23–16	
	South Africa (H)	Centre	W 29–19	
	Canada (H)	Wing	W 33–19	

	Japan (H)	Wing	W 64–15	1 try
	Australia (H)	Replacement	L 9–26	
2000:	Italy (H)	Centre	W 47–16	1 try
	England (A)	Centre	L 12–46	
	Scotland (H)	Centre	W 26–18	
	Ireland (A)	Centre	W 23–19	
	Samoa (H)	Wing	W 50–6	1 try
	United States (H)	Wing	W 35–11	
	South Africa (H)	Centre	L 13–23	
2001:	England (H)	Replacement	L 15–44	
	Italy (A)	Replacement	W 33–23	
	Romania (H)	Centre	W 81-9	
	Ireland (H)	Centre	L 6–36	
	Argentina (H)	Replacement	L 16–30	
	Tonga (H)	Centre	W 51–7	1 try

TOTAL 35 caps. 10 tries. Won 21 Lost 14

Other Wales matches:

1990: Welwitschia (Namibia)	Centre	W 73–0	
1990: Namibia B (Windhoek)	Centre	W 35–18	1 try
1999: Buenos Aires Province	Centre	L 29–31	1 try
1999: USA XV (Cardiff)	Wing	W 53–24	3 tries
2001: Japan Select XV (Osaka)	Centre	W 33–22	

WALES B

1989: France B (Arcachon)	Centre	L 15–28

LIONS

1997: Tour to South Africa 7 matches 1 try

RUGBY LEAGUE INTERNATIONALS

Wales: 12 matches 3 tries
Great Britain: 3 matches

CLUB APPEARANCES

Maesteg: 1984–9	136 matches	50 tries
Neath: 1989–90	75 matches	37 tries
Warrington: 1990–5	142 matches	52 tries
Cronulla: 1995–6	34 matches	7 tries
Richmond: 1996–9	69 matches	27 tries
Northampton: 1999–2000	51 matches	7 tries
Barbarians: 1996 v Australia	1 match	1 try

TOTAL FIRST-CLASS APPEARANCES: 572.
TRIES: 201.